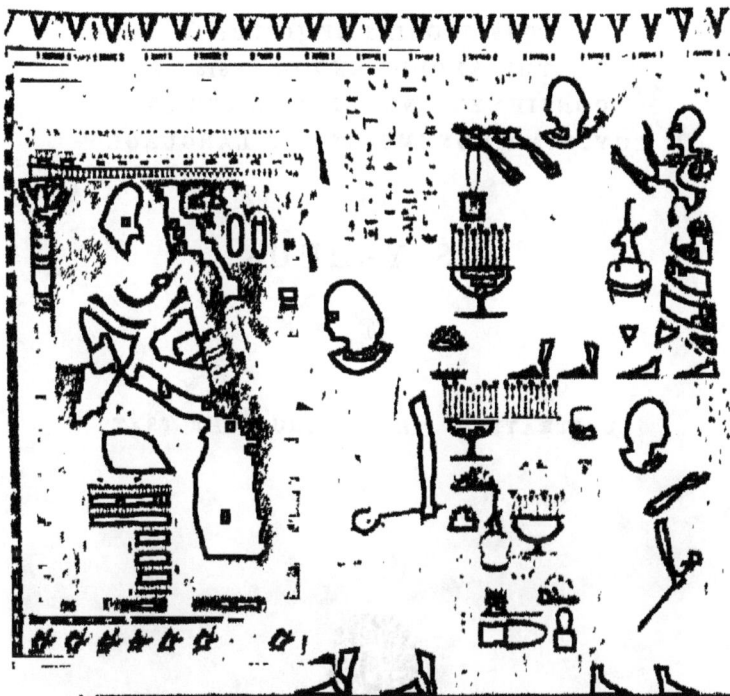

The Pharaoh in audience, invested in gala-robes holding the sceptre, sitting on the throne under a richly decorated canopy, receiving presents and tributes from Asiatic princes introduced by ushers. The Prince heading the deputation is wearing a "coat of many colours" as mentioned in Gen. 37^3 (see page to it and Gen. 41^{46}, 47^2 and 47^7)

THE ACCURACY
OF THE BIBLE

THE STORIES OF JOSEPH
THE EXODUS AND GENESIS
CONFIRMED AND ILLUSTRATED BY
EGYPTIAN MONUMENTS AND LANGUAGE

BY

A. S. YAHUDA

ILLUSTRATIONS THROUGHOUT THE TEXT

1935
E. P. DUTTON & CO., INC.

FIRST EDITION

TO MY WIFE

FOREWORD

THE widespread interest aroused by the two series of articles published by the *Daily Telegraph* in 1932 and 1933 under the title of "The Truth of the Bible," and the persistent demand of a large public to see the articles in book form, induced me to prepare a book on the lines of these articles, but largely amplified by substantial additions and supplemented by a greater number of illustrations.

As the title of the book indicates, its principal object is to demonstrate in a popular way the accuracy of the Bible in describing events and things, and through this the antiquity and authenticity of the Biblical writings. For reasons explained in the Introduction, I have selected 1 the Joseph narrative, 2 the Exodus narrative, and 3 the Genesis stories, for the purpose of the present book, as a forerunner of similar publications extending over other portions of the Bible. This is, however, not done by discussing problems and issues on theoretical or speculative lines, but by expounding the affinities of Biblical accounts and the customs, manners, languages and thoughts of the peoples with whom the Hebrews lived in close contact during the first stages of their early history; more especially with the Egyptians among whom they spent a considerable time (Ex. 12^{40}) until they definitely established their national unity after the Exodus from Egypt.

In taking up the task of proving the Hebrew-Egyptian relationship from a wider and broader angle than has ever been done hitherto, it is not intended to substitute the pan-Babylonistic method of deriving everything Biblical from Assyro-Babylonian sources—a method which was so much in vogue and is still dominating Biblical research—by a similar one-sided pan-Egyptianism.

The author of the present book has considered it as his duty to equip himself, as much as possible, with the knowledge of the languages and cultures of the neighbouring countries and peoples of Israel, a necessity which is not yet sufficiently realised by Old Testament scholars, before he felt justified to come to decisive conclusions about the orientation to be followed in establishing the relationships between the Bible and the surrounding cultures and languages. He has already dealt at length with this problem in his book, *The Language of the Pentateuch in Its Relations to Egyptian* (Oxford University Press, 1932), and substantiated his views and methods with full evidence derived from the documents and monuments themselves and supported by the investigations and statements of most authoritative scholars. Thus following the same principle in the present book the connections of the Biblical narratives with the neighbouring centres of culture have been expounded with equal objectivity, circumspection and caution, by pointing on the one hand to the Assyro-Babylonian similarities, and on the other hand to the subsequent influx of Egyptian elements. As at the same time some features and conceptions could be traced from the

Canaanite Homeland of the Patriarchs, they have been
equally taken into consideration and put in the right
light, so as to complete the picture of the conditions of
life among the Hebrews when they settled in Egypt, and
to show that in spite of having adapted themselves to
the Egyptian environment, they still retained some
typical habits of their homeland (p. 33 seq.).

Of course, the object of all these demonstrations is
not merely literary, historical or philological, but, as
already indicated, chiefly aims at proving through the
tracing of the various relationships and especially
through the establishment of the combined Assyro-
Babylonian and Egyptian character of some of the
Genesis stories, that the Biblical narratives by their form,
their style, their linguistic garb and peculiar colouring
could only have developed in the course of the migrations
of the Patriarchs from Ur through Canaan to Egypt
and the return of the Hebrews from Egypt back to the
Land of Promise.

In some cases I had to point out that the renderings
in the English Bible were either tentative or based on
erroneous conceptions which could only be put right
through the knowledge of Egyptian (e.g., pp. 76, 94,
103 and notes 8, 9, 33.)

In other cases where a strictly literal rendering of the
Hebrew text was necessary for the exact understanding
of the original, I departed from the English version
(pp. 10, 21, 75 seq.). But all this does not mean any
criticism of the English version which, in spite of
the cases mentioned and notwithstanding its obsolete
character in other cases, I still prefer in many aspects

to some of the more modern and "scientific" translations with all the alterations and so-called "emendations" of the original Hebrew text.

As this book is more destined for the general public, I have abstained from an overloading documentation by notes and quotations which most probably would be overlooked by the reader. I only confined myself to a certain number of explanatory notes which are attached at the end. Those who would take a deeper interest in the details may be referred to the afore-mentioned, *The Language of the Pentateuch.*

Before I conclude, I deem it a pleasant duty to express my thanks to the Rev. C. B. Mortlock for some valuable hints in connection with the book, and to the publishers and printers for the solicitude and special care they displayed in printing and illustrating the book.

Hampstead,   A. S. YAHUDA.
       October, 1934.

CONTENTS

FIRST SECTION

THE JOSEPH NARRATIVE

SECOND SECTION

THE EXODUS NARRATIVE

THIRD SECTION

THE EARLY STORIES OF GENESIS

CONTENTS

xvi

PERIODS OF EGYPTIAN HISTORY

1. The Old Kingdom, III-VI Dynasty, from 2900-2400 B.C.
2. The Middle Kingdom, XI-XIII Dynasty, from 2200-1800 B.C. The rule of the Hyksos, the so-called Shepherd kings, begins about 1780 B.C., ending in 1580 B.C., by their expulsion through Ahmose King of Thebes.
3. The New Kingdom, XVIII-XXI Dynasty, from 1580-945 B.C. The XVIII Dynasty ends shortly after Tutankhamon at about 1350. The XIX Dynasty attained the height of its power with Seti I and his son Rameses II between 1350 and 1250 B.C.; the XX Dynasty with Rameses III between 1200 and 1160 B.C.
4. The Saitic period, opening with the XXV Dynasty, dates from just before the end of the eighth century B.C.
5. Later Periods. In 525 B.C. Egypt was conquered by the Persians, in 332 B.C. by the Greeks and in 30 B.C. by the Romans.

The period of the New Kingdom, particularly the time of the XVIII Dynasty, is the most important for us, because it comprises the time of Israel's Bondage and the conquest of Canaan.

The dates given here and in the book are only approximately calculated. With a few exceptions, in which the dates are established on the ground of astronomical evidence (here indicated by a *), historians differ in fixing the dates, in some cases 25-30 years.

The following dates are to be noted (all B.C.):

1580, The expulsion of the Hyksos.
1557*, Amenophis I   ⎫ The Pharaohs of the
1501-1447*, Thutmosis III. ⎭   oppression.
1448*, Amenophis II, the Pharaoh of the Exodus.
1413, Amenophis III, the Pharaoh at the fall of Jericho.
1375, Amenophis IV, Akhenaton, the Pharaoh of the
                              Tell-el-Amarna tablets.
1292-1225, Rameses II.
1225-1215, Merneptah.

INTRODUCTION

The Problem of the Five Books of Moses, and the Creation of the Literary Hebrew Language

THE most important problem which has occupied Old Testament Scholars during the last century has been: whether we have in the Pentateuch—that is the five books of Moses—a unitary work by one man, composed at a definite time, and in the very form and order in which it lies before us; or whether it is a product of various times, extending over many centuries, developed gradually, and reflecting thereby various religious currents and social tendencies.

A minute, but very complicated critical analysis of the whole text, carried along certain lines, chiefly based on tendencies lying outside the Bible and operating with speculative methods of an inductive rather than a deductive nature, has decided a great number of Biblical scholars in favour of the second opinion, and has led to the establishment of the modern school of Higher Biblical Criticism.

THE QUESTION OF ANTIQUITY.—This school proclaimed it almost as a dogma that the latest portions of the Pentateuch could not have come into being before the time of Ezekiel, during the Babylonian exile in the sixth century B.C., whereas the oldest portions are attributed to writers of the ninth and eighth century B.C., the time when the prophetic era reached a high level and a great literary activity was displayed in Israel (Ex. 12⁴⁰).

This view places, therefore, even the oldest portions of the Pentateuch many centuries after the Exodus period, when according to Deut. 31⁹ "the Law" was written down. Thus the Pentateuch is made to appear as the creation of an environment which, both in time and place, was altogether remote from the Egyptian centre of culture, where, according to Biblical statements, Israel had sojourned for several centuries.

Even the more conservative opinion within this school only admits that certain features and traditions have been preserved from ancient times in various parts of the Pentateuch, and that in Deuteronomy there are some elements which may go back to a period more or less close to the Exodus. But, taken as a whole, the hypothesis of the modern Biblical school accepts as a fact that the Pentateuch, as it has come down to us, reflects, both in its contents and its linguistic garb, the product of a long development, beginning with the consolidation of the Kingdom in Israel in the ninth century B.C., and ending in the Babylonian exile in the sixth century B.C. and even later.

There is no necessity to go into further details with regard to the supposed different sources of the Pentateuch, since even those who are not Biblical Scholars have often enough heard about J (Jehovistic), E (Elohistic), P (Priestly), and D (Deuteronomistic) as being the main sources of the Pentateuch. [*See Note* 1, *p.* 217.]

DESTRUCTIVE METHODS OF BIBLICAL CRITICISM.—No one, and the present writer least of all, would make the slightest attempt to belittle the great merits and achievements of Biblical criticism. But it must be said that, so long as moderate views prevailed, there was a sane and sound method in Biblical research. Unfortunately this method has since deteriorated through the more radical views adopted by the modern school of Higher Criticism, especially under Wellhausen and his followers.

The whole system has degenerated into a mass of farfetched hypotheses and haphazard theories, which only fitted within a frame of preconceived ideas about the history, the development and the composition of the Scriptures. In the long run it became customary to consider it as highly scientific to challenge everything Biblical and to alter the texts at one's heart's desire.

The whole Pentateuch is represented as a conglomeration of various sources. In many cases one chapter is attributed to two, three, or more sources. Even in each one of these sources two or more underlayers are discerned. Thus, taking the whole Pentateuch as it is made to appear, the impression is left of a patchwork stuck together by stupid authors and ignorant scribes, the result being a most disproportionate and inharmonious composition.

Indeed, the mania of seeing everywhere a wrong text and detecting all kinds of interpolations, glosses and anachronisms, and likewise the zeal to heap emendations upon corrections resulted in creating a new speciality for speculative "experts" to exert themselves in the art of text alterations and source-hunting.

Even the purely historical records of the Bible are questioned, and the events related in them adjusted to preconceived views by changing the text, eliminating whole sentences as glosses, and adding other sentences by commentators, who very seldom penetrate to the true spirit of the Hebrew language, so that their emendations are very far from being congenial to the Biblical language and style and rather make the impression of being translations of those European languages in which the commentaries are written. Thus the original text was distorted and disfigured and in its place was offered a quite new text of pure invention.

Doubting Biblical statements became a standard of scientific method in Biblical research, and critics practising that method earned recognition and acquired great authority. The greater the doubts raised the more was appreciation expected; and the more numerous the hypotheses brought forward to discredit Biblical statements, the more credit was granted to the scientific soundness and critical sagacity of the sceptics. All these methods and arguments only betray the superficiality with which the Biblical documents are treated by Biblical critics, and indicate their embarrassment in attempting to maintain arbitrary theories which can be proved neither by documentary evidence nor by logical reasoning.

THE RECORDS OF THE EARLY HISTORY OF ISRAEL.—A still more radical standpoint was adopted with regard to the early history of Israel, especially that of the Patriarchs and the sojourn of Israel in Egypt. Indeed the whole story of the Patriarchs was declared as more or less legendary, and that of the sojourn of Israel in Egypt was represented as the product of much later periods containing only very pale reminiscences of vague old memories of the Egyptian epoch, and episodes invented with the object of substantiating later conceptions by earlier supposed events, which according to those sceptics had never occurred.

The notable finds yielded by the excavations in Assyria and Babylonia, which confirm the Biblical records, have been employed rather to shake the authority of the Bible than to uphold it. Because some of the Genesis stories bear a remarkable resemblance to Assyro-Babylonian myths, of which the story of the Great Flood is the best example, it was assumed that they were written during the Babylonian exile, in the sixth century B.C., and that only certain portions were of two or three centuries earlier. Yet, on closer examination of the Genesis stories from a linguistic point of view, I have found that the Assyro-Babylonian traces were much fewer than was supposed, and that those stories can by no means have been composed in the Babylonian exile nor in the ninth or eighth century B.C., but that they must belong to the time of the great civilisation of Ur, in the time of the Patriarchs (see *Lang. of the Pent.*, pp. 104-121).

THE VIEW OF EGYPTOLOGISTS.—Likewise the excavations of Egyptian monuments and documents which, when properly studied, would enormously contribute to the understanding of the Bible and more especially of the Pentateuch, were either ignored or dismissed as negligible.

It is true that such noted Egyptologists as Brugsch, Ebers, Wilkinson, Birch, Naville, Petrie and others, have already, more than fifty years ago, realised the great importance of Egyptology for the Bible, and followed the right path leading to a better comprehension of the relationship between Israel and Egypt. Nevertheless the view of some "representative" Egyptologists remained unchanged.

This view was chiefly based on the statements of the Egyptologists Erman, Spiegelberg, and others who supported Biblical criticism most insistently, emphasising again and again that Egyptology had very little to yield for the advantage of Biblical studies, and that, on the other hand, all that is said in the Pentateuch and other parts of the Scriptures about Egypt could not be looked upon with enough suspicion. [See Note 2, p. 217.]

But from among all Egyptologists however none has gone so far in his efforts to challenge the Biblical accuracy and genuineness as Wilhelm Spiegelberg. He raised himself to the rank of a real henchman of Biblical critics and made it his speciality to prove through Egyptology the correctness of their views about the untrustworthiness and ignorance of the author of the Joseph and Exodus narratives. Even in cases in which his own findings clearly show the intimate connections of the Biblical narratives with Egyptian, he made all kinds of attempts to belittle their importance. He attributed to himself the authority to make the most apodeictic statements in Biblical matters in spite of admitting that he did not feel competent in Hebrew, and that he had to seek guidance and enlightenment from a Biblical scholar who, in his turn, did not know a single word of Egyptian! This very much reminds one of the famous fable of the Lame and the Blind, who, in combined action, proceeded to deprive their neighbour of his figs!

It is necessary to make all this known because, in spite of these facts, Spiegelberg is still held in great honour by Biblical critics and regarded as a highly qualified authority in Biblical-Egyptological questions.

THE JOSEPH AND EXODUS NARRATIVES.—The few relations which *could* be found between the Joseph-Exodus narratives and Egypt were, strangely enough, utilised by them to prove exactly the opposite of that which should actually be proved, and were employed rather to obscure the Egyptian background of the narratives. It was asserted that their author or authors had very little knowledge or none at all of Egyptian matters, and that even such features which, according to their views, still preserve certain Egyptian colouring, had been supplied by tourists or Hebrew mercenaries in Pharaoh's army who happened to be in Egypt! Those people have just snatched a few things from Egyptian life, picked up a few words from the Egyptian language and brought them home for the benefit of scribes who utilised them for literary exercises.

The scientific world was again assured in the most assertive and authoritative manner that the Joseph and Exodus narratives, far from conveying a true picture of an Egyptian environment, were so remote from everything Egyptian that they could serve as the best proof of the imperfect knowledge of the authors, and of their complete lack of acquaintance with Egyptian life and Egyptian conceptions. It is almost an irony of fate that the books of those Egyptologists, who most obstinately reject substantial Biblical-Egyptian relations, are among those which provide the most valuable evidence in support of the astonishing acquaintance of the Biblical authors with the most intimate conditions of Egyptian life. There is also hardly any portion of the Pentateuch for which better and more comprehensive evidence could be brought from the Egyptian monuments and language than the Joseph and Exodus narratives.

As we shall later see, the same scepticism is entertained also with regard to the historicity of the sojourn of Israel in Egypt and the Exodus. Here too some Egyptologists advanced very hazardous views in support of those critics who disbelieve in the validity of the story as a record of Hebrew history.

ARCHÆOLOGICAL AND LINGUISTIC EVIDENCE.—In order to show the exactness of our views it is first of all necessary to make it clear that decisive proof of the genuineness and antiquity of the Joseph and Exodus narratives must be derived from a combination of archæological and linguistic evidence.

It need hardly be emphasised to what a great extent archæology has already proved itself to be a useful and trustworthy source of information and confirmation in Biblical questions. As a matter of fact, the excavations in the countries connected with Israel's history, in Mesopotamia, Syria, Egypt, and Palestine itself, have brought many monuments and documents to light which have served to confirm Biblical statements and to confound Biblical critics.

Moreover the very recent excavations by Mr. Leonard Woolley in Ur have produced fresh evidence of the truth of the Flood story in the Pentateuch; and now the most important of recent archæological discoveries in support of Biblical data is that made by Professor Garstang at Jericho, as we shall later see. This because the walls of Jericho have disclosed a secret which remained for thousands of years buried in their cracks—the secret, namely, that the fall of the walls, hitherto looked upon as a mere legend, was a real historical event, due to an earthquake having occurred just at the time when the Israelites were besieging that city.

ISRAEL'S MIGRATIONS REFLECTED IN THE LANGUAGE.— But archæology without the study of the languages concerned cannot take us very far. The monuments and objects dug up from ancient times, important as they are, are not sufficient to make us fully acquainted with actual life in Biblical times, with the spiritual ideas and cultural values created by the Hebrews in those periods. It is imperative to make a thorough study of the linguistic relations between Hebrew and the languages of the neighbouring countries, and this much more intensively than has hitherto been done. It was this goal that I put before me when I began to seek the truth about the Bible and the people of the Bible. In my search for tracing and establishing such linguistic relations I was guided by the following two facts:

1. During the two thousand five hundred years since

the Babylonian exile, the people of Israel voluntarily or involuntarily led a wandering life; not as an uncivilised nomadic tribe, but as a people, seeking, creating, and transmitting spiritual and material culture did it wander from nation to nation, from land to land.

2. Through all the different periods of Jewish civilisation, it was in the first place the language of the peoples among whom the Hebrews dwelt that exerted the most intensive influence upon them. The Hebrew language, even at times when only in literary and scholarly use, did not cease to live but was continually enriched by the adoption of new elements through close contact with other peoples, and varied cultural surroundings. In the development of·the Hebrew language, one can follow the route of Israel's wanderings during the last twenty-five centuries. In its expansion and enrichment, we can see reflected the fresh cultural values acquired in all periods. All the newly created conceptions, all the borrowed or imitated expressions, phrases and modes of speech, as well as the adopted foreign words, are to be found embodied in the language, and worked into its texture. Thus there are Aramaic, Assyro-Babylonian, Persian, Greek, Latin, and Arabic elements, finally elements from modern languages in their most recent developments. And from ancient oriental times and classical antiquity down to our day, it has not been so much the vernaculars of primitive peoples in Israel's surroundings, but the languages of the most cultivated peoples of the world that have exerted the most powerful and penetrating influence on the Hebrew tongue.

From these facts I was led to argue as follows: If the

Biblical data concerning the wanderings of the Hebrews from the beginnings of their early history, when the Patriarchs went forth from Ur in Southern Babylonia through Aram to Canaan, until the reconquest of the Promised Land after the Exodus from Egypt are correct; and if, further, it is correct that the Pentateuch originated in the Exodus period, just before the return of the Hebrews to Canaan—then it should be possible to discover in Hebrew strong traces of the languages of the lands in which the Hebrews dwelt in those times, more especially in Assyro-Babylonian and Egyptian, then the richest and most highly developed languages on both sides of Canaan.

THE COMMON HEBREW-EGYPTIAN ENVIRONMENT.—Now Assyriologists long ago discovered Assyro-Babylonian elements in the Bible, and established more especially the relation between the Babylonian myths of primeval times and the Genesis stories. Egyptologists have also found a certain number of words of Egyptian origin in the Joseph and Exodus narratives. But my investigations have led me to establish that, on one side, the influence of Assyro-Babylonian was much less than has been assumed, and that, on the other side, the influence of the Egyptian language is far more discernible in the Pentateuch than Egyptologists have ever admitted.

That influence is, indeed, very palpable, not only in the Joseph and Exodus narratives, but even in those portions of the Pentateuch, which most strongly disclose Assyro-Babylonian influence, such as the Flood story; and this is so to such an extent that the language of the Pentateuch cannot be explained except as a new creation of a common Hebrew-Egyptian environment, when the Hebrews lived for a long period in a constant and most intimate contact with the Egyptians.

As there is no other period in which this could have happened than the time assigned by the Pentateuch to the sojourn of Israel in Egypt, this process can only have been the result of a long stay in Egypt itself.

HEBREW AND EGYPTIAN.—If we accept the theory of a common Hebrew-Egyptian environment, it would appear obvious that those parts of the Pentateuch in which Israel is shown to have been in direct contact with Egypt—like the Joseph and Exodus narratives—should display most visible traces of Egyptian influence on the language. This is, indeed, the case in those narratives in which the sojourn of the Hebrews and their experiences in Egypt are described. Here we find that incidentally a great deal of Egyptian life is illustrated with a wealth of detail which could only have been derived from thorough knowledge and exact observation at close quarters. From the very beginning, when Joseph appears in Egypt down to the end of the Exodus story (Gen. 39 -- Ex. 15), we have a vivid picture of the manners, customs and usages of the Egyptians in all walks of life and domains of thought, set out in a language which has likewise absorbed the spirit of Egyptian both in speech and style. This surprising acquaintance, this most intimate familiarity with Egyptian life, is everywhere apparent in both the language and modes of expression. A mere superficial examination of the narratives dealing with

Egypt reveals a whole series of non-Semitic words which have long since been recognised as Egyptian. To these many other words have to be added which are still regarded as Semitic by most scholars, but which in reality are Egyptian. In spite of their foreign origin, their alien nature has so little troubled the Hebrew writer that in one verse alone, Ex. 2³ no fewer than *four* Egyptian words occur. The text referring to the mother of Moses reads:

"And when she could not longer hide him, she took for him an *ark* of *bulrushes*, and daubed it with *slime* and with *pitch*, and put the child therein; and she laid it in the flags by the *river's* brink."

Now the words *tébā* for ark, *gōme* for bulrushes, *sūf* for flags or reeds and *ye'ōr* for river, are Egyptian loan words. In adding that in this portion alone, which is but a fifteenth part of the Pentateuch, no fewer than eighteen Egyptian loan words occur, I think that this fact in itself is quite enough to invalidate the contentions of Egyptologists and Biblical scholars. Such a phenomenon is conceivable only in a time when the Hebrews were in an Egyptian environment, still speaking their own language, but being most intensely dominated by the spirit of the Egyptian language. [*See Note* 3, *p.* 217.]

These borrowings, however, are merely external marks. The true relationship between Hebrew and Egyptian can only be fully appreciated when we penetrate very deeply into the psychology of the Egyptian language, and into the very fibres of its structure. It is only then that we are able to detect, by close comparison, the real meaning of many words, expressions and phrases which occur in these narratives. Only then can we appreciate the whole style and mode of narration as influenced by the Egyptian environment.

It is then that we obtain a complete insight into the intimate and comprehensive knowledge which the author of these narratives, and of the Pentateuch as a whole, possessed of the literary language of Egypt. Only then can we realise how on the other hand his language, though dependent on Egyptian, was able to develop the highest degree of elasticity and individuality, and to display a most fascinating elegance in all its linguistic niceties and nuances. It is in this new orientation wherein lies the real value of my investigations.

THE HEBREWS AMONG THE EGYPTIANS.—As a matter of fact, many details in the Joseph and Exodus stories point to an environment, where the Hebrews lived for themselves, preserving their special characteristics in spite of mixing with the Egyptians. Thus we are told in Ex. 12⁴⁰, that the Hebrews spent a long time in Egypt as a tribe apart (Ex. 1⁹ seq.) with their own manners and specific customs (Gen. 43³²; Ex. 8²²), with their own worship (Ex. 5¹⁷; 8²¹ seq), living in a separate area assigned to them in the Delta near the Asiatic border (Gen. 47⁶ and ¹¹; Ex. 8²² ; 10²³ etc.), and with their own organisation (Ex. 4²⁹) as a self-contained entity in the midst of an Egyptian world. From all these and similar passages it is clear that the Hebrews regarded themselves as an alien people, and that they were so treated also by the Egyptians, not merely in the first period of their settlement, when they were singularly favoured under

Joseph, but at a far later date, when they formed an important and influential but dreaded element (Ex. 1⁹), more especially during the period of their oppression and servitude.

In such a long period the Hebrews cannot possibly have escaped the influence of Egyptian culture and Egyptian life, but must, on the contrary (Gen. 50² seq.; Ex. 1¹⁶) in spite of their segregation, have adapted themselves from the very start to Egyptian conditions, conceptions and customs. The dialect which they brought with them from their Canaanite home could likewise not but keep absorbing Egyptian elements in the course of this period, and in adaptation to the Egyptian have continued to develop, to extend and even to modify its original grammatical form and syntactical structure.

BIRTH AND GROWTH OF THE HEBREW LANGUAGE.—Obviously I can do no more than only allude here to these purely philological questions. For the present purpose it may suffice to sum up in a few sentences the results I have arrived at, which are as follows:

1. The Patriarchs brought with them to Canaan from their migrations from Babylonia through Aram an Aramaic dialect strongly sprinkled with Assyro-Babylonian elements. This influenced the Canaanite dialect, then adopted, inasmuch as reminiscences of Babylonian myths and Assyro-Babylonian expressions reflecting Babylonian conditions passed into the Canaanite dialect.

Through its assimilation by the Patriarchs to their Aramaic dialect, that Canaanite dialect reached a higher stage of development, and began to rise above the level of primitive expression. This was the very moment when Hebrews and Canaanites parted ways, and when out of the Canaanite a separate dialect began to develop among the Hebrews—as the Hebrew language. [*See Note* 4, *p.* 218.]

2. This language was retained by the Hebrews in Egypt, and gradually developed during their stay there under the influence of the Egyptian language. It grew constantly, being expanded, enriched and embellished to such a degree as to create the necessary conditions under which the literary language which we have before us in the Pentateuch could mature and be brought to perfection.

THE HEBREW LANGUAGE AS A GENUINE CREATION OF THE HEBREWS.—As to the relationship between the Hebrew language and Egyptian, the most striking feature is the fact that, in this new linguistic organism created by the Hebrews, the foreign material assimilated from the Egyptian language was moulded and transformed in a genuine Hebrew spirit; and this with a wealth and power of expression, with an elasticity, strength and dignity, which bear an entirely individual stamp. Everything that Hebrew adopted or imitated from the Egyptian in the way of words or phrases, as well as what it owes to Egyptian in grammar, syntax and style, invests this language with a unique character, differentiating it in many respects from all other Semitic literary languages. It will result from the nature of this relationship that Hebrew, as it stands before us in the Pentateuch, was a genuine creation of the Hebrew people, reflecting its migrations from Ur through Aram and Canaan to Egypt, and thence back to Canaan through the Sinai desert and the *Arabah* on the Eastern boundaries of the Jordan. This is the language in which the earliest Hebrew documents were written, as we have them in the Pentateuch. It is this language which became classical for the subsequent Biblical Scriptures, and with which began the whole of Hebrew literature.

THE STORIES SELECTED FROM THE PENTATEUCH FOR ILLUSTRATION.—After these considerations of a more general character, we proceed with the illustration of the Egyptian background of particularly characteristic portions selected from the Pentateuch. It will be shown that in subject matter and form they can only be understood from a common Hebrew-Egyptian environment. We shall, however, avoid discussing purely philological questions.

As in our case the application of the environment theory can only be valued, if it can be proved that the Egyptian influence is most vividly revealed in that portion of the Pentateuch which tells of the life of the Hebrews among the Egyptians, we begin with the Joseph and Exodus narratives. In the course of our demonstration it will be shown by numerous examples that the Egyptian environment is most strikingly reflected in this portion. But, as much has been written about the Joseph and Exodus stories, it may be expressly stated that in some cases we deemed it necessary to deal with details already expounded by other scholars and authors, either by amplifying them or illustrating them from another angle, or finally by commenting on them from a linguistic point of view, so as to make them appear in their true Egyptian light. [*See Note* 5, *p.* 218.]

From these two portions we shall then proceed to deal with that portion of the Pentateuch which tells of primeval times and events, and in which Assyro-Babylonian elements are contained. Our reason for choosing this portion and placing it after the Joseph and Exodus narratives, is of a peculiar significance. Hereby it would namely be possible to show that the Genesis stories must have come to the knowledge of the Hebrews before their Egyptian period, and that these stories have been remoulded in an Egyptian colouring and that consequently such a process can only have occurred in a Hebrew-Egyptian environment.

After alluding to the elements originating from the Assyro-Babylonian environment, it will be shown that all other elements, which are generally admitted to be alien to the Assyro-Babylonian spirit, are of Egyptian origin. Further, that they appear to an overwhelming extent in the most important Genesis stories together with some loan words, idioms and phrases, typical of this portion of the Pentateuch, and finally that there are other highly significant Egyptian features, which provide the background for many conceptions concerning the Creation, the Paradise, the Flood and even the Tower of Babel. The fact that all these elements are precisely those which are foreign to Assyro-Babylonian in matter and in spirit, and further the fact that they are more abundant than the others, makes it in itself evident that they represent later additions, and that consequently the Assyro-Babylonian elements are reminiscences of an earlier date. The establishment of this latter fact is of special importance, as it entails far-reaching consequences for the whole question of the composition and antiquity of the Pentateuch.

All this will contribute to demonstrate that the presence of Egyptian elements in the Pentateuch is the best indication that the Books of Moses have actually been composed in that epoch, in which the Hebrews were still under the immediate influence of their connections with the Egyptians, just as it is stated in the Pentateuch itself.

FIRST SECTION

THE JOSEPH NARRATIVE

CHAPTER I

JOSEPH AND THE PHARAOH

JOSEPH BEFORE HIS ADVENT TO POWER.—No sooner does he start telling the story of Joseph, than the narrator plunges deeply into Egyptian life. He approaches his audience or readers not as one conveying something foreign, something strange, almost unknown, coming from a remote country, but he straightway assumes as a matter of course a complete acquaintance with land and people. Manners and customs are mentioned which indicate, nay, presuppose a thorough familiarity with the structure and manifestations of Egyptian life. Many individual features of social, family and court life just touched upon by him are likely to be passed over by the reader as devoid of special significance. On closer study of actual Egyptian conditions, however, they are found to be intentional allusions to common, very popular occurrences in connection with certain ceremonies or important social and state institutions. By the brevity and casual nature of these allusions, it may be clearly inferred that they could be understood in their full significance only by those who either knew them from first-hand observation, or had themselves at some-time participated in them.

3

JOSEPH'S DUNGEON AND HIS SUMMONS BEFORE PHARAOH.
—The whole incident of Potiphar's wife with Joseph
reveals the Egyptian background with all its local
colouring. There is an Egyptian story of the Two
Brothers Inepu and Bata which provides so many
similarities to our story that it may serve as an illustration
of the whole episode with Joseph. Although such love
affairs could occur in any other country, the charm of the
story lies in its Egyptian background and local colouring.

The great Berlin historian, Eduard Meyer, found the resemblance so striking that he could not conceive the Joseph narrative as anything but fiction, and suggested that it was a mere adaptation of the Egyptian story. Unfortunately he forgot that he belonged to the chorus of those scholars who decried the author of the Joseph narrative as completely ignorant of Egyptian matters. That he could suddenly credit the same author with such a good knowledge of Egyptian literature, is because he did not mind having it both ways as soon as the Bible is involved.

The type of an Egyptian lady of higher rank.

The reference to the dungeon into which Joseph was thrown (Gen. 39$^{20-2}$), makes it clear that it was not an ordinary gaol, but a very special prison for dangerous criminals or political offenders. As I have shown (*Lang. of the Pent.* pp. 38-42), it was in the well-known fortress *Saru* on the borders of the Palestine frontier. As a matter of fact, it is mentioned several times under Thutmosis III (1501—1447 B.C.), and in the edicts of Haremheb (1350—1315 B.C.), as a prison for grievous offenders, just as it appears from Genesis 39²², that it was an establishment for forced labour under the supervision of the chief executioner.

This fortress must be identical with that one mentioned by Sinuhe under Amenemhet (about 2000 B.C.) on the "Paths of Horus." At any rate *Saru* was very well known long before the New Kingdom when the Joseph narrative was written down.

Butlers serving the king and queen and the guests.
From Tell-el-Amarna.

5

As for the butler and the baker, we can refer to some reliefs depicting these high officials "in action." From the one we see the butler pouring a drink in the cup of a Princess while she is undergoing the strain of a hair-dressing toilet, holding a brass looking-glass to follow the work of her hairdresser. In another tomb we see the "chief of butlers" sitting in his vineyard receiving the accounts of the product of his domains. And on one of the reliefs of Tell-el-Amarna is the wonderful scene of the royal butler in his function at the court of Akhenaton.

Other reliefs show a bakery and men carrying baskets heaped with loaves and cakes on the head, exactly as did the chief baker in the presence of Pharaoh.

Royal Bakery from the tomb of Rameses III. (12th Century B.C).

There are other little details which do not draw the special attention of the reader, because of their general character. Thus, for instance, no English reader will find anything unusual in the statement that Joseph was

The butler serving his Royal lady whilst she is having her toilet made (see p 6, l 3 *seq*)

A Royal Prince in robes of finest linen (called *sesh*, the same word as in Hebrew Gen. 41⁴²) similar to the vestures in which Joseph was arrayed when proclaimed as Vizier (see p. 11, l. 7 *seq*)

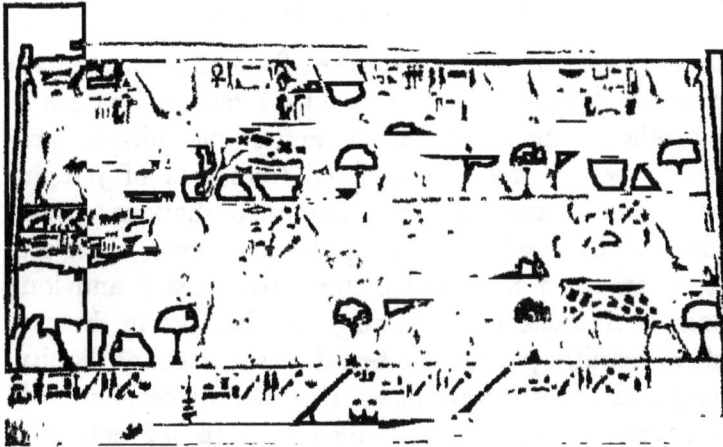

The seven cows of Hathor followed by the sacred bull (see p 8, l 7 seq)

Seven cows grazing in the "Garden of Amon" in the meadow under frankincense-trees (see p. 8, l 13 seq).

shaved, as soon as he was freed from the dungeon. It nevertheless points to a very characteristic feature in Egyptian conceptions of cosmetics and hirsute propriety, which radically differed from that of Joseph's homeland Canaan. For only Semitic barbarians allowed their beard and hair to grow and were, therefore, represented in Egyptian pictures with beard and long hair as characteristic of foreigners. Because in the eyes of all Semitic people the beard was a mark of dignity, long hair an ornament of warriors and heroes, and only prisoners and slaves were shaved as a sign of humiliation and dishonour. The Egyptian had an exactly opposite view and the first thing every Egyptian of better standing was anxious to do, as soon as he came of age, was to deliver his head and face to the razor of the barber. He only grew beard and hair, when mourning for near relatives. Thus Joseph was made to appear before Pharaoh not as a barbarian and in foreign garb but as a well-dressed and well-shaven perfect Egyptian gentleman. [*See Note* 6, *p.* 218.]

Barber using a razor of firestone, otherwise used also for surgical operations (Ex. 4[25]).

PHARAOH'S DREAM.—As to the famous dream of the seven fat and seven lean kine (Gen. 41$^{1-7}$) it was several years ago pointed out by Edouard Naville and others that such a story was only conceivable in Egypt, where the goddess Hathor was worshipped in the form of a cow. And as there were seven districts each having its *Hathor* cow, hence the seven kine. In the tomb of Nefretiry, the beautiful wife of Rameses II, the seven cows are to be seen accompanied by the bull-god, as if they were marching in a solemn procession. In another picture, the *Hathor* cow is seen looking out of a grove of papyrus reeds. In the Book of the Dead the seven cows appear in an offering scene; and on the wonderful mural reliefs of the temple of Hatschepsut in Dair-al-Bahri are to be seen seven cows feeding in a meadow under trees. This is the picture that appeared to Pharaoh in his dream. What, however, so much disturbed him and so much confused his magicians was not the appearance of the seven cows in itself, but the accompanying details, that there were fat and lean kine, that they were followed by seven full and seven empty ears of wheat. The magicians of course could not but think of all kinds of eschatological connections in the nether world. And that was where Joseph's wisdom came in, that he eliminated any connection of the kine with the Beyond, but regarded the whole dream as a prognostication of happenings in the land itself, seeing in the connection with the ears a relation to the food conditions of the country and accordingly interpreted the seven kine and seven ears as "years of plenty" and "years of famine."

8

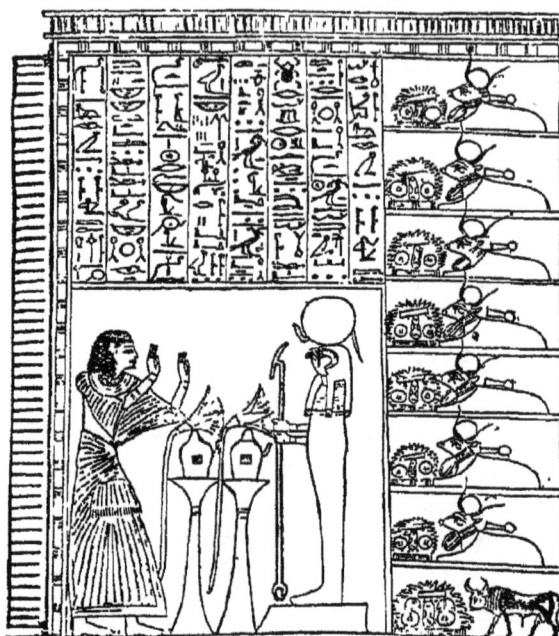

Seven Hathor cows in an offering scene.

Here, too, the language testifies to the close relations between Hebrew and Egyptian. For "years of famine" (Gen. 41[54]) is a genuine Egyptian expression and the Hebrew presents nothing but a literal translation of the Egyptian phrase *reneput-hekeret* "years of hunger." [*See Note 7, p.* 218.] But not only this, the whole conversation between Joseph and Pharaoh bears a thoroughly Egyptian stamp. Thus, quite at the beginning, Pharaoh says (Gen. 41[15]): "I have dreamed a dream, and there is none that can interpret it: and I have heard say of thee, that thou canst understand a dream to interpret it." For '*canst understand*' the Hebrew has 'thou *hearest* a dream.'

9

This corresponds entirely to the Egyptian use of *sedem* "to hear"="to understand," a meaning which is most clearly shown by its use in the phrase "he hears the speech of Egypt," i.e. "he understands the language," exactly as "heard" is used again Gen. 42²³, for *understood* the language.

Even ordinary phrases of deference, such as are or might be in vogue at any court, are here highly typical of Egyptian etiquette, and only become clear in their right meaning in the light of Egyptian court ceremonial and the Egyptian conception of good breeding. A characteristic formula is the phrase recurring in several passages "to the face of Pharaoh" or "from the face of Pharaoh" (for "unto" or "before" Gen. 47 ², ⁷, 41⁴⁶) meaning "in the presence of Pharaoh." This corresponds completely to hierarchic court custom whereby one might not speak to his majesty (*er-heme-f*) but only "to the face of his majesty" (*em her heme-f*, or *hefet her heme-f*).

THE GOLDEN NECK CHAIN.—The particulars given (Gen. 41⁴²) of Joseph's honours which accompanied his installation as vizier, with solemn ceremonies, perfectly coincide with Egyptian usages. They could not be better illustrated than by the Egyptian inscriptions and pictorial representations in tomb reliefs.

The ceremonies at the court of Pharaoh were very complicated and full of pomp and splendour, especially during audiences. The King sat on his throne invested with all his regalia, bestowed on him by the gods themselves on the day of his coronation. A richly ornamented canopy was extended over him, and carpets in gay colourings lay beneath his feet and in front of him. Visitors were introduced to his presence by ushers, holding plumes in their hands as sign of their dignity. This was also the manner in which we may conceive Joseph as being received in official audience (Gen. 41⁴⁶) on the day of his elevation by Pharaoh to the highest office in the State. Dressed in garments of fine linen, which was the distinctive garb of kings and high personages, the royal signet was conferred on him and he was invested with the gold neck chain. The latter was not, as it may appear, a mere present, but a special ceremony showing in a rather spectacular manner the investiture of a high state dignitary, among the plaudits of the people. It was known as the conferment of "the gold of praise," or simply "the Gold."

Seti I (1313—1292 B.C.) on his throne under a canopy, behind him is the goddess of truth, Maat, before him the High-Priest and Vizier, invested with the gold neck chain, whilst addressing the king with a panegyric speech.

11

From earliest times of the Middle Kingdom (2200 B.ς
great army commanders and royal functionaries of hiς
rank craved for this decoration with much the same
covetousness as an English nobleman for the Order of the
Garter.

It consisted of valuable gold jewels presented by the
king to the recipient, among which the chief gifts were
long necklaces of many gold strings. In ordinary cases
these jewels were placed by the keeper of the treasury
at the king's behest round the neck and on the arms and
ankles of the recipient. A similar scene is shown in the
reliefs of Amarna. Here we see Mery-Ra, the "High-
Priest of Aton" in the courtyard of the storehouse of the
temple, invested by the treasury master with the gold
neck chain by order of the King Amenophis IV because,
as it is stated, "he filled the storehouse with spelt and
barley," just as in Joseph's case. But in the splendid
pictures in the tomb hall of Eye, the favourite of Amenophis IV, Akhenaton (1375-55 B.C.), we see a detailed
representation of the ceremony of the conferment of
"the Gold." When this same Eye received "the Gold"
for the second time on the occasion of his marriage with
Teye, the special honour was given him of receiving the
Gold from the hands of the king himself. With special
pomp, Eye and his wife were conducted in two royal
chariots with a royal escort to the palace, accompanied
by numerous fanbearers, servants and troops of runners
in front of the chariot; while whole regiments of Syrian
and Nubian soldiers followed them as bodyguards. No
fewer than ten scribes accompanied the procession in
order that the gracious words which the king would

12

address to him might be carefully recorded. The king, leaning on the gay cushions of the balcony parapet, threw down the Gold upon his faithful servant, and the Queen, with her youngest child in her arms, also threw down gold chains, and the two elder princesses joined her in the display of throwing bracelets. A veritable shower of treasures fell upon Eye and Teye.

The King Amenophis IV on the balcony with the Queen and princesses behind him throwing gold necklaces and other jewels to Eye "father of the god" (the same title as given to Joseph) and his wife Teye standing behind him.

In the first row are the carriages in which they were driven to the Palace

2nd and 3rd row numerous scribes busy registering the amount of jewels given by the royal family.

4th row: Servants and fanbearers watching the ceremony, raising their arms in adoration to the king

5th row: Servants carrying away the heaps of the jewels in their bags.

ROYAL HONOURS AND CEREMONIES.—Here we have a documentary description of the ceremony of the conferment of the gold necklace on Joseph, as given in Gen. 41⁴². Also here Joseph was the recipient of the

13

greatest distinction. For it was the King himself who placed his signet ring upon his finger and put a golden chain round his neck. He also was driven in a royal chariot through the streets with runners calling for attention in front of him. There are many pictures showing royal chariots in sumptuous official apparel, the horses fully caparisoned as on solemn occasions of state ceremonies, or when driving out at the head of the army in battle array. It shows most elaborate crafts-manship, it is inset with gold and engraved with beautiful scenes and figures. This is how we have to imagine Joseph's chariot when he was driven through the land to proclaim his appointment to high office with runners shouting in front of him. Another picture shows the runners on both sides and in front of the royal chariots.

Royal chariot in sumptuous official apparel.

It is noteworthy that some old Egyptian customs have been preserved unto this very day in the valley of the Nile. In the same manner as runners were employed in

14

front of Joseph's and Eye's chariot, so throughout the ages right down to the khedives and viceroys of modern times, runners have been employed to clear the way for kings, princes, viziers and high state personages. Probably Lord Kitchener was the last counterpart of Joseph to have the *sayis* (Arabic word for runner) with swords in their hands running in front of his carriage.

The most amazing thing is that even the expression, which was shouted by the runners in Joseph's time, is still alive in present-day Egypt. This expression was, as we learn from Gen. 41^{43}, "*Abrekh*" which literally means in Egyptian "Mind thee!" in the sense of "Look out! Look out!". Now many people, who happen to have visited Egypt, will have heard in the streets of Cairo animal and vehicle drivers shouting all along the roads to the pedestrians the word "*Balak! Balak!*" which in Arabic is exactly the same as "Mind thee", thus coinciding literally with the old Egyptian "*Abrekh!*". As a matter of fact this is only one of the many expressions and phrases which have come down from Ancient Egyptian into Arabic through the medium of the Coptic language after Egypt was conquered by the Arabs in 642. [*See Note* 8, *p.* 218.]

THE FUNCTIONS OF A VIZIER.—Not only are the ceremonies to which I refer of astonishing accuracy, but also the descriptions of Joseph's function and position as vizier are in full accord with all that we know concerning the duties and privileges of the state officials standing next after the king. In this connection we are particularly enlightened by detailed regulations for the office of vizier preserved in the tomb inscriptions of Rekh-My-Ra, the vizier of Thutmosis III (1501-1447 B.C.). The whole description of his installation into his office is so vividly reminiscent of the Joseph narrative that it can be regarded as an authentic confirmation of the Bible narrative and, even more, as an illustrative commentary on the details furnished by the narrator.

The King and Queen in the Royal chariot. In front of them is the Vizier and his deputy running before the chariot together with the runners   Tell-el-Amarna

After the king, the vizier is the highest dignitary in the State with all the rights and powers accruing to the king. In a word he replaces the king. In the king's absence the vizier is the actual ruler and in the king's presence no person and no matter can reach the king except through the vizier's mediation, just as Pharaoh said to Joseph (Gen. 41⁴⁴): "I am Pharaoh, and without thee shall no man lift up his hand or foot in all

16

the land of Egypt." It is the vizier who issues all orders and he it is who carries out the royal commands. Every officer from the highest to the lowest must report to him. Even in legal proceeding, in complaints by officers against one another, as well as in criminal cases, the decision rests with the vizier as the supreme judge. The signet ring signified not only the confidence of the Crown, but it was also a token of high privilege, the bestowal of which rested with the king alone.

The vizier is furthermore the supreme administrator of the crown lands, the country as a whole being also under his supervision, corresponding with the statement of Gen. 41[40] seq.; "Thou shalt be over my house, and according unto thy word shall all my people be fed," and again, "See, I have set thee over all the land of Egypt" (see also 45[8] etc.). In the hands of the vizier lay the real direction of all affairs in court and state, he being the true ruler next to the king. As it is said (Gen. 41[40]): "Only in the throne will I be greater than thou." [*See Note 9, p. 219.*]

In a picture of Rekh-My-Ra's tomb we can see the high court in which the vizier sat to dispense justice. Before him are the forty law-rolls on two mats. On both sides stand the scribes, ushers and officials of the court and outside are the litigants waiting to be called or dragged in by ushers. There are also pictures showing a vizier wearing signet rings.

CHAPTER II

JOSEPH'S TITLES AND DUTIES

The Royal Son, Vice-King of Kush, receiving the signet ring (Gen. 41⁴²)

As already mentioned, it was the narrator's tendency or purpose to convey that Joseph's installation was in every respect in conformity with all hierarchical customs and laws of Egypt. This is very clearly shown in Joseph's own description of his office and dignities (Gen. 45⁸) which in form and expression are Egyptian, thus complementing what has been said in reference to it, Gen. 41⁴⁰⁻⁴⁶.

In summarising them, he refers to his three functions: (1) as "father to Pharaoh" (2) as "lord of all his house" and (3) as "ruler throughout all the land of Egypt." The threefold nature of the position of a vizier at the court of Pharaoh is thus exactly described, namely (1) as priestly dignitary (2) as court chamberlain, placed over the entire court, and (3) as supreme administrator of the entire land, as we have seen above. Such a precise summary can only have emanated from someone who was intimately familiar with the hierarchic state institutions of Egypt, and knew that these were the most important offices which were embodied in the person of a vizier.

18

"FATHER" TO PHARAOH AND "LORD OF ALL HIS HOUSE."
—The expression "father" is a reproduction of the Egyptian *ity* or *itef* "father," a very common priestly title which was borne by humble as well as very high officers including viziers. Thus we find, e.g., that Ptah-hotep the vizier of King Issy (about 2675 B.C.) referred to himself as *itef neter mery neter*: "father of god, the beloved of god" (A. M. Blackman, *The Lit. of the Egyptians*, p. 56 note 1). Also the above-mentioned Eye who occupied a high office at the court of Akhenaton had the title "father of god" (Davies, Amarna VI, plates 29 and 30) as had many others who were close to the throne. In the statement that it was Pharaoh who installed Joseph as *father* we have implicitly an indication of the Egyptian character of this title. In a hierarchic state where Pharaoh was a god (*neter*), his vizier had naturally to occupy a priestly rank, and it was precisely this which was conferred on Joseph by the title *father*. This qualification was enhanced by Pharaoh giving him the daughter of the priest of On (Heliopolis) to wife (Gen. 41⁴⁵). The narrator was quite clear as to the hierarchic significance of such a union, and of the high position occupied by the priests of On. For to the Egyptians On was the holy city *par excellence*. It was regarded as the seat of the most powerful of the cosmic gods, namely of Atum, and it was occupied by a numerous and important body of priests. Its central sanctuary was established as early as the middle of the fourth millennium B.C. when the first god Ra was already ruling there. The marriage of Joseph to the daughter of the priest of On, therefore, signified the reception of the

for attention: in describing Joseph's reform the writer says (Gen. 47²⁶) that he "made it a law over the land of Egypt *unto this day*." Although this phrase is, as I have expounded elsewhere, not to be taken literally as referring to the time of the author of the story, I must point out that the Biblical critics, who think that it is to be applied to the time of the writer, cannot at the same time challenge the antiquity of the Joseph story and maintain that it could not have been written earlier than the 9th century B.C. [*See Note* 19, *p.* 220.] Once they admit that the conditions described by him were already in existence from the beginning of the 16th century throughout the New Kingdom and beyond that, why should it not be admissible to believe that the narrative was composed in the Exodus time in the 15th century B.C.? As a matter of fact, the author living much later than the time of Joseph would not have said "unto this day" if that law had not prevailed at that time, and what he wanted to convey was that that law originated from Joseph, because he was aware that it was due to Joseph's initiative of old and not an innovation of later times. This can only have been written by someone who knew that the agrarian system existing in his time harked back to Joseph's reform, much earlier than the New Kingdom, and this is in perfect accord with the view that Joseph's reform is to be placed before the Hyksos time, and that, on the other hand, the story can have been written in the New Kingdom, when that law was again in force, as it is actually confirmed by the documents of that period.

Vizier in full official dress with golden chains round
his neck, receiving Asiatic visitors, the ushers serving
as interpreters (see p 16 and Gen 42²³, also Gen 42⁶
and 44¹⁴)

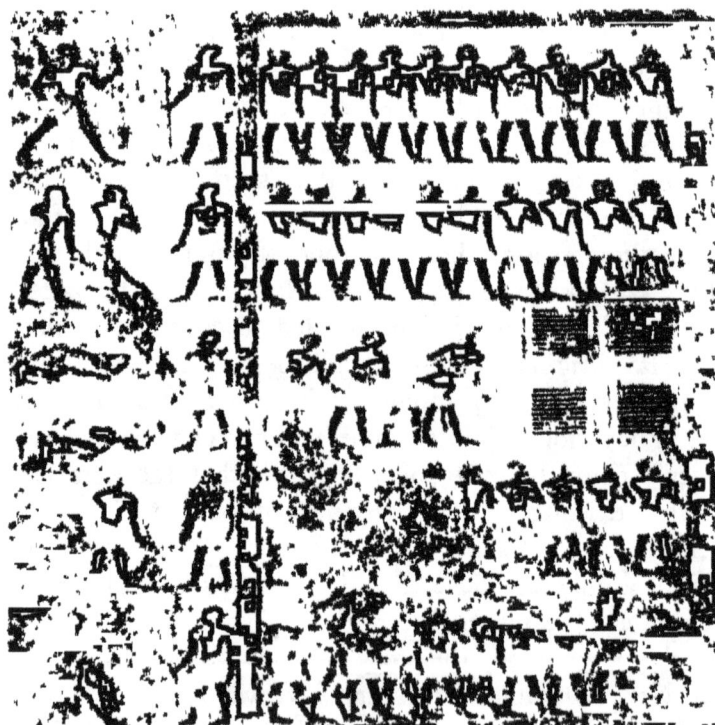

The 40 rolls of the law in four groups in the centre of
the great hall of the High Court on the right hand side
(see p 17, l 20 *seq*).

a matter of fact this is the designation given by the Egyptians to their country from time immemorial, with reference to Upper and Lower Egypt. The origin of the Hebrew word *misrāyim* and its formation are of course purely Semitic, but it is modelled on Egyptian.

The question now arises whether this designation was coined in Canaan, in Aram, or in other neighbouring land from a Canaanite or Aramaic dialect before the entry of the Israelites into Egypt. The fact, however, that in the Tell-el-Amarna tablets of the fourteenth century B.C. Egypt is called *Misri*, or *Missari*, in the singular, and that furthermore we possess no evidence from any other equally early Semitic documents or languages, that Egypt was ever called by a name of dual formation, leads us to conclude that the name *Misrāyim* "the two lands" was an original creation of the Hebrews from the Egyptian *tawy*, as a permanent name for Egypt.

As to the division of Egypt into "two lands," namely a kingdom of "the South" in Upper Egypt, and a kingdom of "the North" in Lower Egypt, it is of a very remote date and had early become deeply rooted among the Egyptian people. The name *tawy* "twinland" always existed, and had always remained the official name for Egypt. One has, however, the feeling that in the use of *tawy* the Egyptians had both lands in mind as separate units, though they applied it to the whole country in general. Such a connotation was already current in the Old Kingdom (2900—2400 B.C.) as well as throughout the whole of the Middle Kingdom (2200—1800 B.C.) and remained still later in use.

THE WHOLE OF THE "TWO LANDS" OF EGYPT.—Now
one has the feeling at the frequent use by the author
of the Joseph narrative of the specific expression "*all*
the land of *misrāyim*," i.e., the "twinland," side by
side with the more general expression "the land of the
twinland," that thereby he intends to emphasise the
fact that in Joseph's time *both lands* were united under
the rulership of Pharaoh and under the administration
of Joseph, as a sign of consolidated power and unified
government. [*See Note* 11, *p.* 219.] Thus the narrator
shows, in this connection too, his complete familiarity
with the changeful conditions in the Nile valley. Hence
his concern to stress the fact of a united Egypt, when he
tells of Joseph's installation over the *whole* country of the
"two lands" (Gen. 41$^{41, 43}$), when he speaks of his extraordinary plenary powers over the *whole* country of the
"two lands" (41^{44}), when he mentions that immediately
after Joseph's appointment as vizier he journeyed
throughout the *whole* country of the "two lands" (41^{46}),
or that he later transferred the peasantry to the towns
"from one end of the borders of the 'two lands' to the
other end" (47^{21}). In this last instance it is particularly
clear that all the territories from the south to north in
both Upper and Lower Egypt were included.

This remarkable emphasis assumes special historical
significance when it is recalled that before the New
Kingdom there was only one vizier for both territories,
and that it was only in the New Kingdom that two
viziers came on the scene—one for Upper Egypt with
the title *tsaat-en-resy*, "Vizier of the South," and the other
for Lower Egypt: *tsaat-en-mehw*, "Vizier of the North."

The author of the Joseph narrative must have known of these changed conditions, and therefore wanted to bring out the fact that in contrast to his own time, when there were two vizierates, Joseph was the sole vizier over the *whole* country of the "two lands." And this he emphasised, not only because it had been the administrative system of that earlier time, but also because of the necessity of preparing for the threatening catastrophe which rendered essential a unified and strong administration of the entire country in the hands of a wise and far-seeing counsellor. For if there had not been such a change in the conditions of the vizierate, and had the narrator no knowledge thereof, he would have simply contented himself with the statement that Joseph was installed as vizier of Egypt, without emphasising on every occasion that the *whole* country of the "two lands" was under his rule. It is consequently not possible to admit that Joseph's appointment was for him a mere legend. On the contrary he records it as a positive historical fact, illustrated by such features as could only be rightly understood and appreciated in the light of changes introduced in state institutions much later than the Joseph period. We have thereby gained an important clue which, together with other indications discussed below, will be of no little significance for a closer delimitation of the epoch to which the Joseph period has to be assigned.

JOSEPH'S EGYPTIAN NAME.—After having commented on the titles of Joseph it is opportune to discuss the question of the origin and meaning of Zaphnath-paan-

23

eah, the name given by Pharaoh to Joseph (Gen. 41⁴⁵). That the name is composed of Egyptian and not Hebrew words, is now generally admitted. It is only concerning the form and meaning of the component elements of the name that Egyptologists differ. That Pharaoh should confer on Joseph an Egyptian name on his elevation as his viceroy was quite natural not only for the purpose of giving him, the foreigner, externally the character of an Egyptian dignitary, but also because on such occasions, even with Egyptians, it was customary for the king to bestow upon a favourite an honorific name denoting a special distinction, and marking at the same time the beginning of a new and important stage in his career. Attention may here be drawn to a particular instance, in which, exactly as happened with Joseph, a Canaanite with the name Ban Yusana of Darabasana, having been elevated by King Merneptah, son of Rameses II to a high office at court, assumed or perhaps was given the name "Rameses in the Temple of Ra," and in addition also the cognomen "the beloved of Heliopolis." In the case of Joseph it is expressly stated that it was the king himself who bestowed on him that name obviously as sign of his admiration and esteem.

THE FEEDER OF THE "TWO LANDS."—We need not enter here into a minute philological discussion of the component elements of Joseph's honorific name. Different explanations have been offered but none of them is so adequate or fits so well in the circumstances in which that name was given, as the interpretation I have suggested (*Lang. Pent.* pp. 31-5) namely, *dzefa-n-ta Pu-*

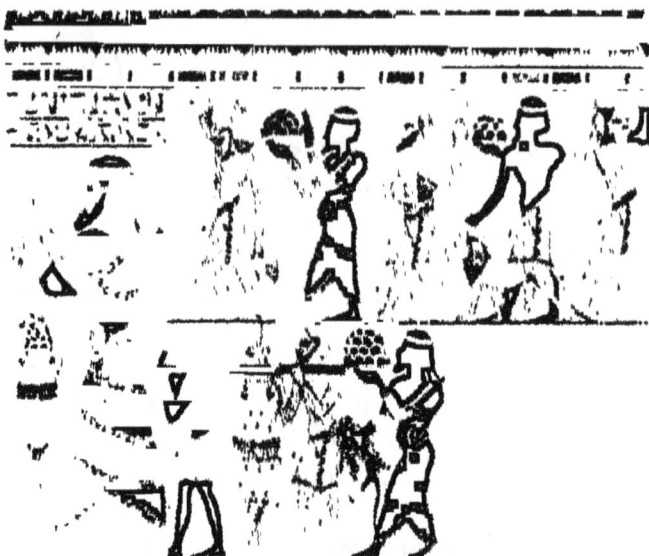

Semitic princes and notables in multicoloured raiments offering
presents and tributes to the King (see p 26 *seq* , Gen. 43^{26} and
Num. 13^{33}).

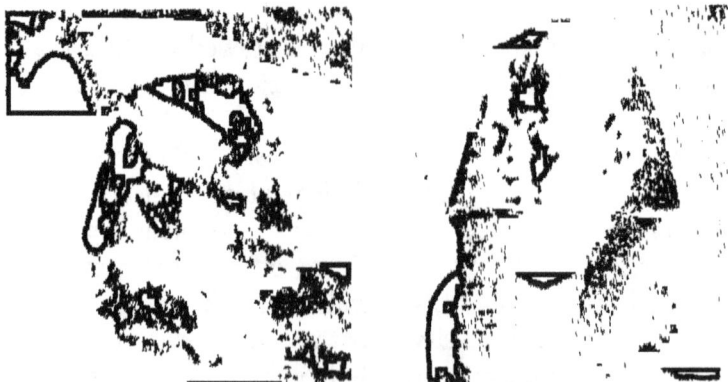

Heads of Shepherd Kings (see p. 45 *seq.*, and p. 51, l. 9 *seq.*).

Anekh, "Food of the land is this living one," conveying the idea that Joseph was the "feeder" of Egypt. This is in literal accordance with Gen. 42⁶ where Joseph is characterised as the *mashbīr* which means "the feeder, nourisher," and is the equivalent of his Egyptian name. This conception is substantially supported by the fact that the idea of the king being the feeder of the land was very current both in royal names and in praising phrases applied to the kings. Thus it is said of Amenophis IV that he was "the food of Egypt," which offers a direct parallel to Joseph's name. In the nineteenth century B.C., a king of the thirteenth dynasty actually bore the honorific name *Saankh-tawy* "Feeder of the two lands," and the first element *dzefa* of Joseph's name was frequently contained in princely names of the thirteenth and fourteenth dynasties. [*See Note* 12, *p.* 219.] This fact is particularly significant for determining the period in which the conferment of such a name on Joseph was popular. That was shortly before the advent of the Hyksos rule in Egypt, and would, as we shall see later, exactly coincide with Ex. 12⁴⁰, extending the time of Isarel's sojourn in Egypt over a period of more than four centuries.

CHAPTER III

JOSEPH AND HIS FAMILY

OFFERING PRESENTS TO JOSEPH.—There are many more features, phrases, idioms and expressions in the Joseph story which can be illustrated by the Egyptian monuments. I could give a running commentary to all the chapters dealing with Joseph, from Egyptian life and customs; but I will mention here only a few of them.

Gen. 43[11] we read: "And their father Israel said unto them . . . take of the best fruits in the land in your vessels, and carry down the man a present, a little balm, and a little honey, spices, and myrrh, nuts, and almonds," and further 43[25-6]: "And they made ready the present . . . and when Joseph came home, they brought him the present which was in their hand into the house, and bowed themselves to him to the earth."

From this passage it appears clearly that they prepared to offer him the present in a solemn manner. As a matter of fact, we know from the Egyptian monuments, that the etiquette would not allow any foreigner to make a present to the vizier of the king without the observance of the prescribed ceremony. Such a scene can be found in a picture in which Canaanite notables are offering presents or tribute to the king in their characteristic Semitic garb. This offers an illustration of the manner in which Joseph's brethren brought before him their father's presents.

In this picture there is, by the way, another detail which illustrates the passage Numbers 13[23], where it is said of the spies sent by Moses to Canaan:

"And they came unto the brook of Eshcol, and cut down from thence a branch with one cluster of grapes, and they bare it between two *upon a staff.*"

PHARAOH'S WAGONS FOR JACOB.—Gen. 45[19] we read that Pharaoh commanded to Joseph to send wagons to Canaan for his old father and the women and children. This is not to be regarded merely as a generous act of courtesy on the part of the King, but as a very fine trait in the ruler who was desirous of sparing his minister the

Semitic caravan, men with short, women with long coats.

embarrassment of letting the families of his brethren enter Egypt in the Asiatic fashion as depicted in Egyptian reliefs, the men riding on asses and the women carrying their children on their backs or arms following on foot. It is expressly stated that Pharaoh took the initiative in this matter and that Joseph was commanded to act accordingly. Hence the Egyptian picture of a nomadic caravan, which Egyptologists and Bible commentators so often reproduce, to illustrate the journey of Israel and his children to Egypt, is a most incorrect representation. The Joseph family at Pharaoh's behest should enter the country in wagons as distinguished members of the vizier's family and were to be regarded as civilised people.

THE FIVE GARMENTS FOR BENJAMIN.—It is noteworthy that, only subsequent to this command, the narrator tells us of Joseph presenting his brethren with "changes of raiment" (Gen. 45, ²²⁻²³) which, of course, were cut in the Egyptian style and not in the Semitic fashion checked in too vivid colours. It is only now that we understand why this was not told before Pharaoh's command. Even such an apparently insignificant remark, that Benjamin was bestowed with *five* "changes of raiment," has a typically Egyptian touch, as this number was regarded by Egyptians as a special distinction. Thus we read in the story of Wen-Amon's mission to the King of Byblos that among the presents sent to him by the Egyptian ruler Smendes, there were *five* suits of garments of excellent upper-Egyptian linen and *five* pieces of the same linen. (See also p. 61).

JACOB BEFORE THE PHARAOH.—In the scene so wonderfully described in Gen. 47 [7-10], we see the old Patriarch greeting the King and offering him his blessing. When asked by Pharaoh about his age, he replies: "the days of the years of my sojournings are a hundred and thirty years: few and evil have the days of the years of my life been, and have not attained unto the days of the years of the life of my fathers in the days of their sojournings." [*See Note* 13, *p.* 220.] In the first place it must appear strange that Jacob describes his hundred and thirty years as few. When, however, we consider that Pharaoh was regarded as an eternally living god endowed by the gods "with millions and myriads of years," being as such praised and worshipped, it becomes clear why the venerable old man had to assure Pharaoh, who was certainly much younger, that his hundred and thirty years were but few in comparison with the endless years of the eternally living son of Ra. Furthermore the remark that his age was not so high as that of his fathers must have appeared to Pharaoh in the light of Egyptian court etiquette as both tactful and thoughtful, especially from the mouth of a foreigner; for it belonged to the good manners of obsequious court visitors to assure the king that they had been given a long life and that many happy years had been theirs because they had the good fortune to enjoy his royal protection and favour. Thus the wise Ptah-hotep, the vizier of King Issy (about 2675 B.C. or earlier), said at the end of his book of wisdom: "It is not little that I have done upon earth: I have lived a hundred and ten years which the king granted me with rewards exceeding those of my fathers because I did what was right for him." Also the statement that he lived a hundred and ten years granted under the auspices of the king has its significance. As a matter of fact a "hundred and ten years" were considered in Egypt as the limit of full age. Now it will be understood why it is said of Joseph (Gen. 50[26]) that he lived a hundred and ten years.

THE PATRIARCH'S HEAVY EYES.—In Gen. 48[10] it is said of Jacob, that his eyes were dim because of his great age. The Hebrew text reads literally: "and Israel's eyes became heavy for age." This remarkable expression which only occurs in the Joseph narrative, and has no parallel in other Semitic languages, is an exact reproduction of the Egyptian expression *denes* "to be heavy," used in connection with the eyes in the sense of being weak and dim, in consequence of great age. Just as in this case, Sinuhe, the Chief Chamberlain of the Queen-mother of Sesostris III (1887—48 B.C.) complaining of his senile diseases, says: "Weakness has overtaken me, *my eyes are heavy*, my arms weak, and my legs do not follow." It is obvious that the use of "heavy" in the same sense and for the same occasion, cannot but be an adaptation of the Egyptian mode of speech. The same word for "heavy" is also used in another metaphor in connection with "heart"; thus we read: "and Pharaoh's heart was heavy" for hardened of the English Bible, Ex. 9[7], also 7[14]; 8[32]; 9[34]: "And Pharaoh caused his heart to be heavy." In all these cases we have an exact literal coincidence with the

30

Egyptian, *denes* "to be heavy," which in conjunction with *ib*=heart means "to be of fixed heart, fixed mind, to be resolved, obstinate, with firm determination". As a contrast the Egyptian characterised the frivolous, the vacillating as being "light of heart." Thus "heavy of heart" means to be stubborn, insistent, to show forbearance, patience, endurance. That is what all these passages convey: Pharaoh did not despair, he was patient, steadfast, resolved, and obstinate in his refusal to allow the Hebrews to leave.

EGYPTIAN MOURNING FOR JACOB.—In Genesis 50²⁻⁴ the narrator describes the preparations *for the burial of Jacob*. From all the details, in spite of their brevity, we can see how perfectly he was acquainted with Egyptian embalming procedures, mourning customs, and funeral

Swathing and wrapping a mummy.

arrangements. Thus the statement (Gen. 50³) that forty days were needed for the embalming of the body and that the Egyptians mourned seventy days for Jacob, exactly accords with the period customary for embalming and mourning in the case of highly placed deceased persons. Shorter periods of mourning were only observed in cases where the position or means of the family of the deceased did not permit such great expense. Just on this account the narrator emphasises that for the father of the viceroy the longer period of seventy days was decreed. [*See Note* 14, *p.* 220.]

It is of great significance that also the expressions here used are modelled exactly on Egyptian phraseology. Thus it is said (Gen. 50²) that Joseph commanded his "*physicians*" (*rōfe'im*) to embalm his father. This expression agrees exactly with the term *seyen* "physician" employed by the Egyptians to denote the embalmers. Similarly the Hebrew expression "days of *weeping*," for days of mourning (Gen. 50⁴) reproduces the Egyptian expression *herwu-en-remy* "days of weeping," for the time observed for mourning. Its Egyptian origin is denoted by the fact that it only occurs in connection with Jacob's mourning in Egypt and nowhere else in the Bible.

During the "days of weeping" there was an extraordinarily elaborate programme of mourning processions with wailing women crying aloud, rending their garments and tearing their hair. The mourning programme also comprised very complicated ceremonies in which various priests took part. Further it is said (Gen. 50⁴⁻⁵) that Joseph asked the "house of Pharaoh" to speak to Pharaoh on his behalf to obtain leave for burying his father in Canaan. This also agrees exactly with the Egyptian custom according to which mourners, however high their position might be, should not approach the King before the burial of their dead.

THE FUNERAL CORTEGE WITH HORSEMEN AND CHARIOTS. —That Joseph did not hesitate, after having devoted

32

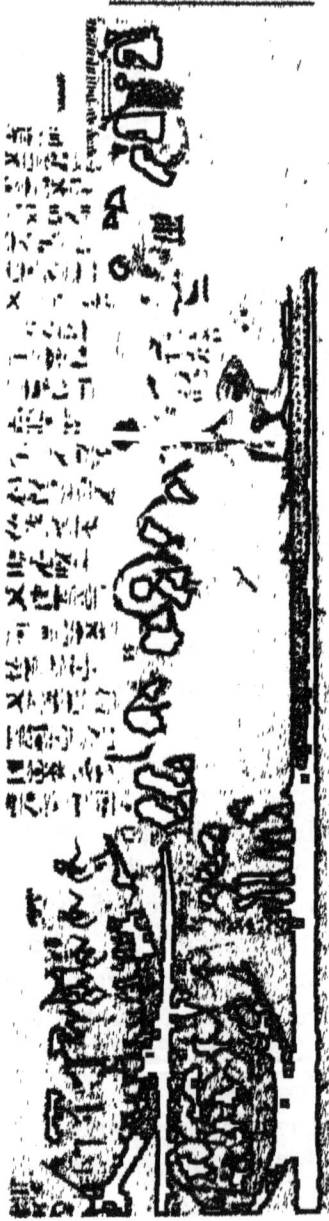

Egyptian funeral scenes on the way to the burial place, notables, wailing women and men accompanying the convoy and priests (with shaven heads) offering to the soul of the dead (see p. 31).

seventy days to mourning, to be absent from his office for a further long period, and to undertake a long journey to Canaan, was not likely to annoy Pharaoh. For in Egypt it was quite customary to convey the dead to distant burial places and to devote long periods to mourning. Also the statement (50⁷⁻⁹) that the cortège was joined by a whole galaxy of high dignitaries, by horsemen and chariots, corresponds to the Egyptian custom of accompanying funeral processions to the burial place in large bands. As a matter of fact, in no other country but Egypt were funerals converted into most elaborate processions, and the interment ceremonies carried out with the greatest pomp, in the case of highly situated personages.

That the death of a king brought the whole life of the State and all public activity to a standstill, went without saying, as the entire people devoted itself for months to mourning ceremonies and those of any status at all vied with one another to participate worthily in the funeral ceremonial and to equip the tomb with valuable gifts. How faithfully the narrator transmits all details, emerges from the enumeration of the classes of officials which escorted the procession to Canaan. Thus (Gen. 50⁷) the "servants of Pharaoh" were the court officials who formed a sort of bodyguard of the King and stood nearest to him; the "elders of his house" are identical with the *shemesu— hayit* which means "the elders of the hall," and who held high court rank. In the "elders of the land of Egypt" we have to understand the high councillors representing all districts of Egypt who had seats in the supreme council of the King. The chariots and horsemen were

33

known to the Egyptian army in the New Kingdom when the Joseph story was written and, as we shall show, must have been known much earlier in the time of Joseph. All these details could only be familiar to a writer who lived among the Egyptians and knew the rules of court etiquette and the gradations of state officialdom.

CHAPTER IV

PATRIARCHAL HABITS RETAINED BY THE HEBREWS IN EGYPT

A VERY striking feature in the Joseph story is the frequent allusion to customs and manners peculiar to the Hebrews and alien to the Egyptians. The very fact that the narrator referred to them as a matter of course with the same brevity and obviousness as he refers to the Egyptian life and manners (see p. 3 and p. xxxii), suggests that he was conscious of addressing himself to people who knew the habits and customs of their country of origin. This is very remarkable as it is an indication that the Hebrews were still reminiscent of their own old habits of Canaan in spite of their having spent considerable time in Egypt and having adapted themselves to the new environment.

THE COAT OF MANY COLOURS.—The following examples illustrate the combined nature of the Hebrew-Egyptian environment as reflected in the Joseph story.

Right at the beginning we are told that Jacob made for his favourite son Joseph a "coat of many colours" (Gen. 37³). Here the traditional interpretation of that rare Hebrew word *passīm* has preserved the true conception the old Canaanites had of rich attire consisting of garments with great profusion of vivid colours, such as

35

are shown in the reliefs depicting Asiatic princes offering the royal gifts to the Pharaoh (see Frontispiece).

TAKING THE OATH.—In Gen. 47²⁹ it is said: "And the time drew nigh that Israel must die: and he called his son Joseph, and said unto him, If now I have found grace in thy sight, put, I pray thee, thy hand under my thigh, and deal kindly and truly with me; bury me not, I pray thee, in Egypt: but I will lie with my fathers, and thou shalt carry me out of Egypt, and bury me in their buryingplace."

This manner of taking the oath was not used in Egypt, but was a custom which is still preserved among the Bedouin tribes in the boundaries of Southern Palestine, where the Patriarchs have lived. The old Patriarch asked Joseph in his last will to swear to him not in the Egyptian fashion, alien to him, but in the traditional manner so as to inspire him with more confidence that his desire would be complied with.

"BORN" UPON HIS KNEES.—Another characteristic trait is the statement Gen. 50²³, where it is said that "the children of Machir, the son of Manasseh were brought up upon Joseph's knees." But the Hebrew text has "were born upon Joseph's knees." This is perfectly right and in complete conformity with the Semitic custom still alive among various Arabian tribes according to which the father receives the new-born child on his knees. This idea is also to be found in Job 3¹², where he speaks of his birth and of "the knees which received" him. [*See Note* 15, *p.* 220.]

36

THE MOURNING AT THE THRESHINGFLOOR.—The most remarkable reference to Canaanite habits in opposition to Egyptian customs is made in the account of Jacob's burial ceremonies. We have seen how accurate are all the details given by the narrator about the burial customs of the Egyptians. Now we shall see how well-acquainted he was with the Canaanite mourning ceremonies too.

After the embalming of Jacob's body and the performance of all Egyptian mourning ceremonies, the body of the Patriarch was taken to Canaan to be buried with his fathers as he requested. The convoy was accompanied by a very numerous and distinguished concourse and we are told that when the company reached the threshingfloor of Atad, on the other side of the Jordan a great mourning was begun which lasted seven days. It is clear that it was the intention of the narrator to inform us that after the Patriarch was given a solemn funeral according to Egyptian ritual, a great mourning was arranged for him as soon as the convoy reached the place beyond the Egyptian border, where it was possible for the Children of Israel to perform the ceremony in accordance with the customs of their homeland. So far, the matter is very clear; but there is one detail which astonishingly enough escaped all Biblical students, though it is of the greatest significance because it gives us the keynote to the whole meaning of the ceremony, and this is the special mention of the threshingfloor. in connection with the mourning outside Egypt. This becomes clear from the mourning customs still preserved in those parts of the borders of the Arabian desert where the stability of life-conditions goes back to very ancient times. Thus in Syria, in *Haurān* on the Anti-Lebanon, where many habits and even words and phrases are so old that some of them remind one of Biblical times, we find that the most distinctive honour bestowed upon a great citizen was to carry his remains on a threshing board accompanied by the whole population of the village to a threshingfloor, which usually lies on the top of a hill, to arrange there for a great mourning which takes exactly seven days, carried out with all the customary tumultuous scenes, with women crying and tearing their hair, men sitting round the bier, beating their hearts, clapping their hands, and uttering loud lamentations mixed with panegyrics in praise of the deceased. [*See Note* 16, *p.* 220.] The threshingfloor is held in great esteem as the place where the heaps of corn loom in the eyes of the villagers in harvest times as a blessing from heaven, providing food and happiness. It is, therefore, considered as the place of honour for a great villager, and the threshing board is used as a bier symbolical of the work and aims of a villager and labourer just as the shield symbolises the martial virtues of a great soldier.

This is exactly the manner in which Jacob was honoured by his folk as soon as they arrived at the first threshingfloor which they met on their way home. It is this and only this that the narrator wanted to convey by referring to the mourning on the threshingfloor of Atad.

Also his observation on the impression which that mourning made on the Canaanite population (Gen.

38

50^{11}) is very noteworthy. The remark that the Canaanites called these obsequies an "Egyptian mourning" does not mean that the Canaanites regarded it as Egyptian in manner and fashion. On the other hand it cannot be possible that the Egyptian ceremonies would be repeated in a foreign land. It was not the ceremony itself that struck their attention; what amazed them was the fact that the mourners were Egyptians. It is obvious that Joseph and the great number of the high Egyptian officials in his company, as well as also his brethren, appeared to the Canaanite population as Egyptians. The Canaanites could not but wonder that Egyptians, who looked upon everything Asiatic with the greatest contempt, should observe Asiatic mourning ceremonies. This would exactly be the case only fifty years ago, that namely Palestinian Arabs would regard their compatriots living in Europe, and wearing European attire, as being *Franjees* (Europeans).

As one can see, the mention of the threshingfloor is not accidental, but intentional for the purpose of making it known that the Patriarch was given at home a funeral in full conformity with the usages of his own country in spite of his son having become the highest Egyptian State official.

BEYOND THE JORDAN.—As to the location of Atad as being "beyond the Jordan" (Gen 50^{10}), it cannot be decided how the expression "beyond the Jordan" is to be understood in this connection, as we do not know the exact site of Atad. Logically it must be supposed that it was situated in Canaan, near the district where the patriarchs lived before leaving for Egypt, that is, on the western side of the Jordan in Southern Palestine. Otherwise the ceremonies could not have been witnessed by the Canaanites, the inhabitants of *"the land"* which can only mean Canaan. This would lead to the further supposition that this remark originates from someone who was writing on the east side of the Jordan, that is, in the *Arabāh* in the Transjordan from whose standpoint Canaan lay "beyond the Jordan" on the east side. It would further imply that it was written before the entry of the Hebrews into Canaan. Without drawing any definite conclusion we may say that this argument has more weight than the attempt made by Biblical critics to consider the remark, "beyond the Jordan," as conclusive proof of their contention, that it can only mean the eastern side of the river, and that hence the narrative must have been written in Palestine, many centuries after the Exodus.

CHAPTER V

The Historicity and Period of Joseph's Appointment

One of the strongest contentions against the historical validity of the Joseph and Exodus narrative, is the fact that neither the king who appointed Joseph nor the kings who oppressed the Hebrews are mentioned by name. The designation Pharaoh, it is argued, is not a proper name; it really means "the great house," and was originally applied to the royal palace and then used as a title for the King of Egypt, just as Czar or Sultan. This argument is strengthened by the circumstance that, in the historical books of the Bible, the names of the kings of Egypt are actually added to Pharaoh. Thus, for instance, Pharaoh-Nechō (II Kings 23[29]; Jerem. 46[2]), Pharaoh-Hophra = Haibra (Jer. 44[30]), or without Pharaoh, as, for instance, Shishak = Sheshonk (I Kings 11[40]), or Zerah = Osarkon (II Chr. 14[9]). It is maintained that had the Joseph and Exodus narratives been written by contemporary authors, the names of the Kings of Joseph's and Moses' times would undoubtedly have been mentioned. This seems to be a very reasonable argument against the credibility of these narratives as historical records. But in fact the opposite is the case.

41

PHARAOH AS THE PERMANENT DESIGNATION OF THE
KING.—It has long ago been noted by many Egyptologists
that in the Egyptian literature it was customary to speak
of the king as "Pharaoh" without mentioning his name.
By a great number of examples from the Egyptian
literature it can be proved that it was precisely in the
New Kingdom (1580-945 B.C.) that the proper name
of the king was given only in solemn inscriptions or in
purely historical records, and not in popular stories of
the kind of the Joseph and Exodus narratives. Even in
royal edicts, in judicial reports and in general records,
the king is simply alluded to as "Pharaoh."

A mere perusal of Egyptian records, tales and narratives of that period makes this perfectly clear, and a good
example is offered in the story of the Two Brothers,
originating from the 18th century B.C., and beginning
with a similar story to that of Joseph and Potiphar's
wife. Here Pharaoh is almost always used for the king,
as can be seen from the following instances. "The
scribes and learned men of Pharaoh were sent for, and
they said unto Pharaoh," etc., "thou wilt be laden with
silver and gold because thou leadest me to Pharaoh";
"and Pharaoh loves him much," etc.; "Pharaoh had
great pity for him," etc.; "the princess rode on horseback
behind Pharaoh," etc.; and similarly in many other
passages. Likewise in ordinary letters of the New
Kingdom the proper name of the reigning king is
omitted, as for instance, "May Pharaoh have regard
for thee," etc.; "it is well with me and with the land of
Pharaoh it is well." Also in the trial of the Harem
conspiracy against Rameses III (1198-1167 B.C.) as

well as the trial of the tomb robbers under Rameses IX (1142-1123 B.C.), Pharaoh is almost the only mode of reference to the reigning king, so e.g., "the scribe of the chief superintendent of the treasure house of Pharaoh," or "the herald of Pharaoh," or "the late Fathers and Mothers of Pharaoh," or "I write concerning them to Pharaoh, my Lord, that a man of Pharaoh may be sent."

The same is the case as in the edict of Haremheb I. There we read of the vegetables of the kitchen of Pharaoh; the taxes of Pharaoh; the houses of Pharaoh; the chief overseer of the herds of Pharaoh; and so on. In all these instances, to which many more could be added, we have exactly the same use as in the Joseph story: "the officers of Pharaoh" (Gen. 40⁷); "the cup of Pharaoh" (40¹¹); bakemeats of Pharaoh" (40¹⁷). Likewise "the house of Pharaoh" (45¹⁶) for the royal residence corresponds exactly to the Egyptian *per-per-a* "house of Pharaoh," a designation which was current in the New Kingdom.

THE OMISSION OF THE KING'S NAME.—It should be expressly observed here that the interchange of Pharaoh with "king of two lands (Gen. 40¹,⁴¹,⁴⁶; Ex. 1¹⁵, etc.), likewise completely corresponds to the usage in the Egyptian narratives of the new kingdom. In conclusion it is worth while pointing out that also among the Assyrians in the Rameside period, and later Pir-u=per-o= Pharaoh was used as a name in the same way as in Egyptian and in the Pentateuch.

The fact that the omission of the king's proper name

was typical for the time of the new kingdom, is particularly important as it was the period of Israel's sojourn in Egypt and most probably the time when the Joseph and Exodus narratives were composed or even written down. The Joseph and Exodus narratives are therefore in full accordance with the literary usage of that time and it results that the omission of Pharaoh's name far from being an argument against, it is rather a proof in favour of their genuineness and antiquity.

It is obvious that authors writing for readers who were presumably aware of the names of the kings in question did not consider it necessary to mention them expressly by name. In other cases they may not have cared about their names,· thinking it was altogether irrelevant for a story to make the names known.

Similarly the author of the Joseph and Exodus narratives either had in mind readers who lived in a time and in an environment where it was not necessary to mention the names of the kings, or he passed them in silence because, after all, he was writing a story and not history; also was his interest more concentrated in the Hebrew than in the Egyptian part of it. On the other hand it was perfectly in order that the chronicler of later times, living in the land of Israel away from Egypt, recording historical events, should mention the name of Pharaoh just as they mentioned the names of the kings of other neighbouring lands, like Moab, Aram, Tyre, and other countries like Assyria, and Babylonia; this for the simple reason that he could not assume that the names of these kings would be known to everyone.

This reason being in itself sufficient, there is an ther

very remarkable fact that after the fall of the 20th dynasty (about 1100), long after the Exodus, the custom of referring to the king merely as "Pharaoh" passed out of usage. Thus in many hieratic documents of the 22nd dynasty (945-745) coinciding with the beginning of the kingdom in Israel, "Pharaoh" or "king" of Upper and Lower Egypt is followed by the name of the king, exactly in the manner in which Pharaoh is mentioned in the books of Kings from Solomon's time onwards. Thus just as II Kings 23[29] and Jer. 46[2] speak of "Pharaoh Necho, King of Egypt," or Jer. 44[30] of "Pharaoh Hophrah, King of Egypt," so the Egyptian Annals of that time refer to the very same Pharaohs. This shows that also in this case the Biblical chroniclers were in complete conformity with a usage which became current in Egyptian historiography.

There is hardly another more characteristic example of the self-reliance and, I may say, pharaonic stubbornness of the exponents of such arguments with the object of discrediting the veracity and genuineness of Biblical narratives! Without even attempting to refute or to explain the facts brought against them, they continue maintaining their contention in a most authoritative and categorical tone and manner peculiar to people convinced of their own infallibility.

JOSEPH AND THE HYKSOS, OR SHEPHERD KINGS.—As to the time of Joseph's installation as vizier, those scholars who do not reject the whole story as a fiction think that it was under the Hyksos, or Shepherd kings, who came from Arabia to Egypt and ruled over it for some considerable time. I do not propose to embark upon a thorough discussion of the question here, and only want to deal with it generally.

According to Ex. 12[40] the sojourn of Israel in Egypt was of 430 years' duration. In fixing the date of the Exodus at about 1415 B.C., that is, 480 years before the building of the temple by Solomon (I Kings 6[1]), it results that Joseph's story began at about 1880 B.C. The view held by some scholars, based on Manetho's history, that the Hyksos or the Shepherd Kings, as they are commonly called, were over 500 years in Egypt, is now discarded, as it is established that their rule began about 1780 and ended 1580 B.C. Accordingly Joseph's appointment must have been long before the Hyksos came to rule over Egypt (see further, p 128).

Although I am not in a position to fix the exact date of the Joseph period, I do not hesitate to state that not one of the arguments advanced in favour of putting the Joseph period under the Hyksos rule can hold its ground in face of the conditions known to us from those times, and that moreover all the facts referred to in the Joseph story clearly point to an epoch when Egypt has been under the control of a purely Egyptian king.

It is very astonishing that the exponents of the Joseph-Hyksos theory should quote Gen. 43[32], where it is said that "the Egyptians might not eat bread with the Hebrews; for that is an abomination unto the Egyptians," in support of their views. If that happens under the Hyksos rule it would be inexplicable that they should allow the oppressed Egyptians to treat their Semitic kinsmen as outcasts. But this is perfectly natural under

46

an Egyptian ruler. Every touch in the Joseph story indicates the tendency to emphasise the alien character of the Hebrews to the Egyptians, which can only be understood under a purely Egyptian ruler.

Besides this, the reluctance of Egyptians to feed with aliens was not, as it is maintained, because of the contempt they had for shepherds. As a matter of fact, the ritual restrictions existed in Egypt long before the Hyksos, and the prohibition of swine and sheep dates from the earliest times and is based on purely Egyptian mythological conceptions connected with episodes from the fighting of the gods against each other to secure world domination.

It may be added that the ritual restrictions were only confined to the priests. But as almost all the Egyptian officials of some prominence had a priestly title, the Egyptians who ate with Joseph and his brethren must have been of a higher rank, otherwise they would not mind eating with the Hebrews. The deference observed towards Joseph, by setting food for himself, was in accordance with the purely Egyptian court etiquette, quite independently of the presence of the Hebrews.

THE ABOMINATION OF THE SHEPHERDS—As a further argument for locating the Joseph period under Hyksos rule, Gen. 46[34] is quoted, where we are told that Joseph advised his brethren to say to Pharaoh that they were shepherds so as to obtain from him the land of Goshen for their dwelling, "for every shepherd was an abomination unto the Egyptians." But how it is possible to maintain that Joseph in his attempt to persuade a shepherd king to allow his brethren to settle in Goshen, would choose such an argument as that shepherds were an abomination to the Egyptians, goes beyond every logical reasoning. Apart from the consideration that this would mean an affront against a shepherd king, one would think that a Semitic ruler should have had every reason to settle kinsmen in the heart of Egypt so as to increase his influence and power, and not to have them settled just on the edge of his country on the Asiatic boundaries.

But the whole idea that the abomination of the shepherds referred to the Hyksos is utterly wrong. Much earlier than the Hyksos rule, and even under the 12th dynasty when there was not a trace of a foreign domination in Egypt, shepherds were an abomination as much as under the later dynasties. Thus this circumstance can by no means be used as a mark for chronological delimitations and cannot have any effect on the date of the Joseph or Exodus narratives. The narrator of the Joseph story in stressing the point only wanted to make it clear that Joseph did not desire his brethren to live among the Egyptians so as not to expose them to the contempt to which the shepherds were at all times subjected, and that on the other hand it was for him a good pretext for asking Pharaoh to allot to them a separate district near the Asiatic border, where there were also other foreign colonies and the antagonism between them and Egyptians was not so sharp.

POTIPHAR "THE EGYPTIAN."—Moreover, the argument that the express mention (Gen. 39¹) of Potiphar being an

Egyptian could not be explained otherwise than from the
time of Hyksos rule is very shaky. First of all, if the fact
be considered that there were always Nubians, Libyans,
Madzyu and other foreigners with Egyptian names employed in military services, it would not be surprising at
all that the narrator should point out the fact of the chief
executioner having been an Egyptian. [*See Note* 17,
p. 220.] But in reality this statement does not mean to
emphasise the strange circumstance that the chief executioner in Egypt was an Egyptian and not, as would be
expected, one of the Hyksos men; it rather stresses the
extraordinary fact that the high official who entrusted the
whole administration of his house to an Asiatic slave, who
in the eyes of an Egyptian appeared as an untrustworthy
barbarian, was a true Egyptian, so as to convey the great
prominence given to a foreigner and thus make Joseph's
position appear in a brighter light. This is only intelligible
from a time in which the Egyptian dignitary served under
a purely Egyptian dynasty, and not from the Hyksos time
when an Egyptian would only be the exception.

Imagine that a French writer supposed to have lived
in the 16th century recorded the fate of a poor French
refugee in England by saying that he found employment
in the house of an Englishman who was a high dignitary
at the court and that he won for himself sympathy and
confidence of his master to the extent of being entrusted
with the entire administration of his house. The statement that he was an Englishman would only mean to
emphasise the distinction bestowed upon a foreigner by
an Englishman. No one would use such a remark as a
proof that that event could have happened only at a

time when England was under the rule of the Normans, four centuries before.

There are many other indications adverse to this theory. One of the strongest proofs against it is the fact that Joseph was given the daughter of the high priest On (Heliopolis) as a special distinction on the part of Pharaoh (Gen. 41⁴⁵). This would be impossible under the Shepherd kings, who did all they could to destroy the Egyptian religion and to weaken the power of the priests, as we shall presently see. Furthermore, the bestowal of a purely Egyptian honorific name on Joseph (Gen. 41⁴⁵) would be inexplicable from a Semitic Hyksos ruler to a Semitic vizier, but is very natural from an Egyptian king to a foreigner appointed to the highest post of the state.

THE ABSURDITY OF THE JOSEPH-HYKSOS THEORY.— These arguments would be quite sufficient to undermine the whole Joseph-Hyksos hypothesis. But there are more fundamental facts which indicate the whole baselessness of this theory. How is it possible to maintain that Joseph's advent to power in Egypt was under a Hyksos rule when in the whole of the Joseph story it is emphasised again and again, on every occasion, that Pharaoh was the ruler over the whole of Egypt, and that when Joseph took the control over the state, the whole of Egypt was subjected to his rule, and that all the measures taken by him to provide the country with food during the years of hunger were applied to the whole of Egypt? The stress laid upon "the whole of Egypt" in the typically Egyptian wording, namely, "the whole of the two lands," can only mean that the whole country, Lower and Upper Egypt, were united under the rule of one king. Now this cannot possibly have been in the time of the Hyksos, because they never extended their rule over "the whole of Egypt," as they were practically confined to the Delta, being in constant conflict with the legitimate more or less independent native chieftains.

Even under the reign of Apophis and his successor Khyan, who are considered as the greatest and most powerful kings, the Hyksos retained their foreign character in spite of Khyan's efforts to adapt himself more than any other Shepherd king to Egyptian manners and views, adding to his royal name all the traditional titles of the Pharaohs. The suggestion that he extended his rule over the whole of Egypt and even beyond its boundaries is derived from indirect indications without documentary proofs. There is no substantial reason whatsoever for believing that in his time the southern part of Egypt, with its centre in Thebes, was not under the control of indigenous Egyptian kings as before and after him.

Besides this, Joseph's advice to his brethren to ask Pharaoh to give them the district of Goshen, in the Delta, near the Asiatic border, can only have a proper sense in a time when the seat of the dynasty was outside the Delta; this could not be the case during the rule of the Hyksos, as the seat of their domination was Avaris, a city in the Delta itself, very near to Goshen.

THE HOSTILITY OF THE HYKSOS TO THE EGYPTIAN RELIGION AND PRIESTHOOD.— Also the concessions granted to the priests in the hunger year (Gen. 47²⁶) could only be undertaken under a purely Egyptian administration. The statement that the whole country was the property of the crown, with the exception only of the lands of the priests, has a very important bearing on the whole question. The supporters of the Joseph-Hyksos theory simply explain this fact by arguing that the Hyksos thoroughly adapted themselves to the Egyptian customs and to the Egyptian spirit. But this view is strongly challenged by the Egyptian reports themselves in which the Hyksos are openly accused of having destroyed their temples, smashed their gods, exterminated their priests and persecuted the Egyptian religion with the greatest severity, instituting the worship of Seth as the central figure of their cult. Now considering that the Osiris religion dominated the whole of the country of Egypt, many centuries before the Hyksos, that Seth was the most abhorred god of the Egyptians, as the arch-enemy of Osiris, because he killed him in order to retain for himself the domination of the world, the substitution of Osiris by Seth, as the highest divinity, must have been felt among the Egyptians as the greatest affront and challenge to the Osiris religion. This offence was, however, not purely religious, but also of very high political consequences, because the whole struggle

Osiris, the god of the dead.

52

between Seth and Osiris was for the purpose of securing universal domination, and the subsequent campaign of Horus, the son of Osiris, against Seth, had the object of recovering from Seth the rule over Egypt and the whole world. Hence the triumph of Horus and the definite defeat of Seth signified the definite establishment of the kingdom of Horus. From that moment Seth was cast out once and for ever, and Egyptian rulership was secured for all time to Horus and his legitimate heirs, the kings who succeeded him on the throne of Egypt. It is from this fact that the Egyptian kings derived their exclusive hierarchical rights. The ban on the religion of Osiris by the Hyksos and their replacing him by Seth meant nothing else but the annihilation of the foundation of the rights upheld by all previous dynasties and the putting up of their own claim as followers of Seth, who remained the only heir of the great gods after he killed Osiris.

How is it, then, imaginable that the Hyksos would recognise the old rights of the Osiris priests and allow Joseph to make them concessions of such importance?

Taking all these considerations together, we cannot but come to the conclusion that the Hyksos not only did not assimilate themselves to Egyptian life and Egyptian spirit, as it is alleged, but that, much to the contrary, they had done everything to offend the Egyptians in their innermost religious feeling and to deprive the ruling classes of their political rights, so that

Seth as the Egyptians conceived him.

the Hyksos fully deserved to be regarded by the Egyptians as "the plague of the land."

THE HORSES AND THE HYKSOS.—In conclusion let us consider another strong argument launched against the possibility of a pre-Hyksos period of the Joseph story. It is the mention of horses (Gen. 47^{17}) and horsemen in the convoy of Jacob's funeral (50^9). It is contended that horses were not mentioned before the New Kingdom in the 16th century B.C. But even in the event that the Egyptians did not use horses in Joseph's time, such an argument would not at all affect the genuineness and historicity of the Joseph narrative, as no one, not even the most conservative supporter of the antiquity of the Pentateuch, suggests that that narrative was written before the 16th century B.C. Now supposing, as I do, that it was fixed in the form in which it is now before us, at the time of the Exodus in the 15th century B.C., it would be only natural that the author should have described the funeral of Jacob having in mind scenes and ceremonies popular in his time.

Seth-Sutekh in foreign representation

The amazing part of it is, that this contention is advanced by those who maintain that the Joseph story could in no case have been composed before the 9th century B.C., that is, five centuries after the horse was already known in Egypt according to their own statement! Thus one would expect that this fact should be used by them rather as a proof that the narrative *could* have been written as early as the time of the Exodus.

Fortunately in this case too the facts are more in favour of the narrator than of his detractors. The recent discovery by Sir Flinders Petrie of a horse skeleton in Gaza from as early a time as the 25th century B.C., makes it evident that the horse was known in Southern Palestine many centuries before the Hyksos rule in Egypt. It would be very strange, indeed, that the Egyptians, who were so near to Gaza, and who from time to time made incursions into Palestine, should not have had any knowledge of the horse before the 16th century B.C., and that it should have taken the horse a thousand years to cover the narrow space from Southern Palestine to Egypt. Thus one would hardly miss the mark in supposing that the narrator was much better acquainted with the hippological conditions many centuries before him in Egypt, and that horsemen could very well be present at Jacob's funeral. [*See Note* 18, *p.* 220.]

Considering all the above-mentioned facts, and adding to them that the Egyptian name Zaphnath-paaneah given to Joseph (see page 25) was characteristic of the 13th and 14th dynasties, in the 19th and 18th centuries B.C., we cannot but conclude that the advent of Joseph to power must have happened before the Hyksos invaded Egypt about the beginning of the 18th century (1780) B.C. As we shall see later, this would very well fit into the calculation of the date of the Exodus in accordance with the Biblical statement (Ex. 12⁴⁰, and I Kings 6¹) and with the fresh evidence brought forward by the recent excavation in Jericho (see further pp. 123 and 128).

CHAPTER VI

Joseph's Land Reform

RURAL CONDITIONS BEFORE AND AFTER THE HYKSOS.—
All the reports about land tenure in ancient Egypt
confirm the existence of a feudal system, whereby the
whole land was owned by barons having the peasantry
under their control. It was only in the New Kingdom,
after the expulsion of the Hyksos at the beginning of
the 16th century B.C., that the whole land was expropriated and transferred to the crown and declared as
the exclusive property of Pharaoh. This law remained
in force during the whole of the New Kingdom (1580-
945 B.C.) and maintained many centuries beyond that.
All these facts are authentically established and un-
reservedly admitted by all Egyptological authorities,
whether they do or do not adhere to the views of
Biblical critics. The statement (Gen. 47$^{20-26}$) that
Joseph *bought* the whole land for Pharaoh, can obviously
only apply to a time when the land did *not* belong to
Pharaoh. Hence this measure taken by Joseph, to have
a state control over the crops, must be regarded as a
reform introduced by him before the New Kingdom,
and the writer must have been perfectly aware of the
conditions which prevailed before the advent of Joseph
to power.

Of course one is tempted to ask whether that reform

could not have taken place during the Hyksos rule in Egypt (18th-17th century B.C.), as from the Carnarvon tablet we learn that "the great men of the Council" in their endeavour to appease the wrath of Khamose, King of Thebes, and champion of the war of liberation, they said that they were quite satisfied with the Hyksos, because they let them keep their lands in Upper Egypt and their pasture lands in the Delta. This proves that under the Hyksos a feudal system was again in existence, so that the *purchase* of the land could very well apply to that time. But as we shall see later, there is one argument which overthrows all attempts to allow such a suggestion, and this is the undeniable fact that the Hyksos only controlled a part of Egypt, leaving almost the whole of Middle and Upper Egypt in the hands of vassals, so that there could not be any talk of *the whole land being the property of Pharaoh*, as during the whole of the Hyksos period there was not one Hyksos-Pharaoh who ruled over the whole of the land of Egypt, as it is constantly emphasised in the Joseph story. The Joseph reform can therefore only have been possible before the invasion by the Hyksos, and when we see that under the Hyksos the land was in the hands of vassals and barons, it means that the feudal system was restored again. Consequently we have in the abolishment of the feudal system and the appropriation of the whole land by Pharaoh in the New Kingdom, not the introduction of a new law, but the reintroduction of the agrarian reform carried through by Joseph and interrupted during the Hyksos rule.

Here mention may be made of a remark which calls

57

for attention: in describing Joseph's reform the writer says (Gen. 47^{26}) that he "made it a law over the land of Egypt *unto this day.*" Although this phrase is, as I have expounded elsewhere, not to be taken literally as referring to the time of the author of the story, I must point out that the Biblical critics, who think that it is to be applied to the time of the writer, cannot at the same time challenge the antiquity of the Joseph story and maintain that it could not have been written earlier than the 9th century B.C. [*See Note* 19, *p.* 220.] Once they admit that the conditions described by him were already in existence from the beginning of the 16th century throughout the New Kingdom and beyond that, why should it not be admissible to believe that the narrative was composed in the Exodus time in the 15th century B.C.? As a matter of fact, the author living much later than the time of Joseph would not have said "unto this day" if that law had not prevailed at that time, and what he wanted to convey was that that law originated from Joseph, because he was aware that it was due to Joseph's initiative of old and not an innovation of later times. This can only have been written by someone who knew that the agrarian system existing in his time harked back to Joseph's reform, much earlier than the New Kingdom, and this is in perfect accord with the view that Joseph's reform is to be placed before the Hyksos time, and that, on the other hand, the story can have been written in the New Kingdom, when that law was again in force, as it is actually confirmed by the documents of that period.

THE LEVY OF THE "FIFTH" AND THE CROP SEASONS.—
In addition to that, also the statements that the fifth
of the crops was to be levied for the Pharaoh (Gen. 47²⁴);
that the land of the priests was not included in the
crown land (47²²), and that they were also exempted
from the fifth (47²⁶), are fully confirmed by Egyptian
evidence.

But there is another detail which lends credit to the
writer of the narrative and which can only be explained
from the agrarian conditions of Egypt. It is said (Gen.
47²⁴) "and it shall come to pass *in the increase* that the
fifth should belong to the Pharaoh." Now inasmuch as
the fifth is concerned, the sense is perfectly clear; but
what is not quite clear is the Hebrew mode of expression
for "the increase," referring to the yield of the land, a
difficulty which has always been felt but not successfully
removed. Moreover, one is tempted to raise the question
whether the "increase," or better, the "crops," comprise
all the products of the field, including vegetables and
fruit like melon and others of this kind; or are we to
understand that only cereals were subject to the fifth?
For the Hebrew expression *tebu'oth* when standing for
"increase," as it does here, generally means grain
crops.

In order to establish this, it must be stated that in
ancient Egypt, as in all subsequent times, the fields were
not sown with wheat every year but alternately one
year with wheat, the second with barley, spelt, rye, or
greens like onions, and the third year it was usually
left fallow. Thus the Egyptians distinguished: a year
of wheat, a year of barley, and a year of grass, which

means a fallow year. In some parts there were two crops in one and the same year, as is still frequently the case in Upper Egypt. [See Note 20, p. 220.]

Now in stressing the word *tebu'oth* the narrator wants to convey that only grain crops and no others were to be taxed with the fifth, thus exempting the yield of vegetables and other products of the field, though the land belonged to Pharaoh. It seems that even vineyards and orchards were likewise exempted as their crops could not be included in the Hebrew expression. This meant a considerable concession in favour of the farmers and peasants. In adding that by Joseph's action the peasants were freed from the yoke of their skinning landlords, it becomes obvious that he appeared to the peasants as a great benefactor, so as to arouse their enthusiasm to the extent of making them utter their gratitude in the effusive terms (Gen. 47[25]), "Thou hast saved our lives: let us find grace in the sight of my lord, and we will be Pharaoh's servants."

PEASANTS AND PRIESTS.—Here too the Hebrew narrator proves to be a better judge of the reform introduced by Joseph than some of the critics who represented Joseph as an exploiter, because he not only expropriated the peasants of their land but still imposed upon them the obligation to pay a fifth to Pharaoh. Gunkel, one of the pillars of Biblical criticism, in his commentary on Genesis, even complacently interprets the words of the peasants as a scornful comment by the Hebrew narrator on the simpleness of the Egyptian peasants who allowed themselves to be taken in by the dictator and, on top

60

of it, melted away in exuberant thankfulness, sub-missiveness and servility. [*See Note* 21, *p.* 221.]

Also the statement that the priests had their require-ments of food assigned to them by Pharaoh (Gen. 47^{22}) is confirmed by Egyptian documents. Thus Rameses III allotted 185,000 sacks of wheat yearly to the priests, and almost all the temples had large tracts of land for the exclusive benefit of the priests. In many tomb inscriptions, too, it is stated that land property was bequeathed to the priests for the upkeep of the monu-ments, and that it was prohibited to sell or to use them for any other purpose for all eternity, millions of years. Thus the words (Gen. 47^{22}), that the priests *did eat the portions* which Pharaoh gave them, exactly refer to the food for the maintenance of the priests assured to them by Pharaoh for all time.

THE NUMBER FIVE. In connection with the fifth it may be noted that the number five seems to have been a basic figure of some importance in Egypt, as has already been observed above. It is very remarkable, indeed, that this figure often occurs in the Joseph story. Gen. 43^{34} Joseph gives Benjamin five times as much as to any of his brethren; 45^{22} he gives him five changes of raiment; 47^{2} he took five men from among his brethren to present them unto Pharaoh. Moreover, we find that Moses ordered as punishment for involuntary appropriation of holy goods the addition of a fifth of the value to the priests (Lev. 5^{16} and Num. 5^{7}); the same punishment for eating unwittingly from holy foods (Lev. 22^{14}); the fifth is also to be added when redeeming holy property whether cattle (Lev. 27[13] and [27]), houses (27[16]), land (27[19]), or the tithe (27[31]). The figure five is of prominence also in some other cases (see e.g. Lev. 27 [5, 6]); also the fifteen (Lev. 27[7]) and fifty (Lev. 27[3]). From all this and other cases it may be gathered that these figures are not merely accidental and that they have some connection with the use of these figures by the Egyptians and the Hebrews.

SECOND SECTION

THE EXODUS NARRATIVE

CHAPTER I

THE FINDING OF MOSES

THE most pathetic episode by which the whole Exodus narrative is dominated, is the story of the child Moses. That the name *Mosheh*, the Hebrew form of Moses, was of Egyptian origin, has long ago been recognised. It was suggested that it is the same Egyptian element *mes* as in many theophorical names, like Thut-*mes* (Thutmosis) or Ra-*mes* (Rameses), meaning Thoth or Ra has given birth, or born from Thoth or Ra.

It is thus assumed that the name was originally preceded by the name of a god like the above-mentioned names, but was dropped out of monotheistic considerations. Other Egyptologists thought that it was identical with *mesy*, "the born-one" in the sense of boy, child, whereby the anonymity of the foundling should be emphasised.

"THE CHILD OF THE NILE."—But apart from phonetical and other difficulties, both interpretations miss the point altogether, because it is expressly said (Exod. 2[10]), "and she called his name *Mosheh*: and she said, Because I drew him out of the water." Now as we know from Egyptian, "the water" was the common expression for the Nile, and it is actually used in this sense several times in Hebrew, in the Exodus narrative (Exod. 7[15]; 8[20]). It is then obvious that there must be in the name itself an allusion to the water, i.e. to the Nile. As a matter of fact, *sheh*, which is the second element of the name, is a very common word in Egyptian, meaning "pond, lake," but was also applied to the Nile, especially to the broad expanses of it, such as that near Fayyum. There can be little doubt that this is actually meant here, and this is precisely the element which provides the link between the name and the Nile. As to the first element *mu*, it was used as a selected metaphorical expression for "seed" in the sense of son, child. Thus *mu-sheh* simply means "the child of the Nile." It was indeed the intention of the narrator to convey that the choice of the name by Pharaoh's daughter for the child was to preserve the memory of his being found in the Nile. It is this feature which had to be emphasised in the name and nothing appears more plausible and adequate than *mu-sheh*, a name meaning "child of the Nile."

And not only the name, but the whole episode, is so permeated with the Egyptian local spirit and the whole colouring is so thoroughly Egyptian, that it could not happen and not even be invented, as some critics suggest, in any other country but Egypt.

BEHIND THE THICKET IN THE BULRUSHES.—We are told (Exod. 2³) that the mother took for him an ark of bulrushes, put him therein and laid the ark in the reeds at the river's brink. Here the narrator had in mind one of those thickets studded with huge and high reed, that were to be seen along the banks of the Nile. It was such a thicket that was chosen by the mother of the

Royal garments as worn by queens
and "daughters of Pharaoh" (see
p 67, l. 7 *seq*)

A thicket on the Nile (see p 68)

From the ruins of the store-city Pithom (see p 73 *seq*)

Brick making, measuring the bricks, supervising the workmen. A supervisor holding a stick, another a flail (see p 75 and p 76, also Ex 5[13-14] and [8]).

child, because it would be only such a sheltered place
that a great lady like Pharaoh's daughter would use
for bathing in the Nile.

Such a place was called by the Egyptians *Sūf*, as in
Ex. 2³, and it was such a thicket of reeds where the
ark was laid.

It may be added that also the expression *bāth par'ō*,
"the daughter of Pharaoh," is not, as generally conceived, the designation for *a* daughter of Pharaoh, but
is a literal reproduction of the Egyptian *saat nesu*,
"daughter of the king," which was the official title of
a princess of royal blood, just as *sa nesu*, "son of the
king," was the official title of royal princes. Thus the
narrator wanted to emphasise that it was the royal
princess who came to the child's rescue. Otherwise he
would have simply said "one of Pharaoh's daughters."

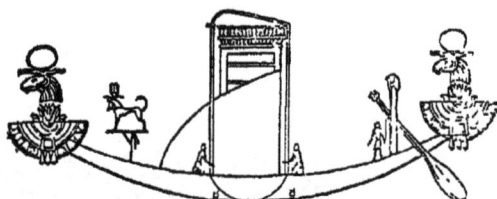

The type of the Ark of Moses as a shrine containing a
divine figure when carried in procession

THE ARK OF MOSES.—Now let us see what sort of an
"ark" was denoted by *tēbā* and how did the mother
contrive the rescue of her child by using just this particular ark? It has long been established that *tēbā* "ark" is
the Egyptian *debet* or *tebet*, and the word has been already
fully discussed. But here its real meaning is coffer, chest,

67

holy shrine, coffin. Such a chest generally had the form of a naos, and served as housing for images of gods which were dedicated to the temples. Of the numerous shrines which have been preserved, several are in stone, others in plain wood, according to the prominence of the deity represented, and the pecuniary means of the donors. The simpler ones, given by humbler people, were in the form of a longish chest, with a door in the front for the statuettes of the gods. On certain festivals, the shrines with the deity figures were borne in solemn procession or carried on the Nile from one temple town to another, on a bier which was usually given the form of a barque such as was conceived as vehicle for the Sun-god Ra and the other gods.

Just such a shrine is to be understood by *tēbā*. The mother had devised a means of saving her child which was peculiarly conformable to Egyptian conditions. She placed the infant in a chest which was exactly in the form used for enshrining images of gods, and laid it among the bulrushes at the spot where Pharaoh's daughter was accustomed to bathe at a certain hour. Her hope was that the princess would, at the first glance, suppose it to be a chest containing the image of a god, that had fallen from a boat into the river and drifted ashore, and that she would have it rescued forthwith. To be sure, the discovery of the strange find might arouse in the princess disappointment or even indignation; in that case the child would meet with the inevitable fate of all Hebrew boys. On the other hand, the effect might be different, and the maternal heart trusted in the divine protection, and not least in the royal pity and compassion. The boy's sister was to stand sentry "to know what would be done to him" (Ex. 2⁴). The princess appears with her maidens. On descending to the river she espies the ark in the rushes, has it brought to her, and discovers a weeping child therein. She divines at once the ruse of the unhappy mother; her heart is touched and thrilled by the thought that the Hebrew woman had trusted in her tenderness and she takes up the child. His sister, now convinced of the benevolent intention of Pharaoh's daughter, and confident that the boy will not be thrown into the river, runs up to the princess with the enquiry whether she may not summon a Hebrew nurse such as was easy to procure among the Hebrews, as there were so many mothers whose children had been thrown in the river. The scheme succeeds in all details—the boy is saved, the royal protection is assured. The boy was given back to his own mother and later, after being weaned, he was taken to the palace where, as the adopted son of Pharaoh's daughter, he was reared with the other royal children.

As will be seen, the narrative reflects ideas and conditions only conceivable in an Egyptian milieu, while the use of the Egyptian word *tēbā* provides the key to the understanding of the whole episode.

THE FINDING OF SARGON.—As it has become customary to invoke a similar legend of the birth and exposure of Sargon I, King of Akkad (about 2600 B.C.) as the probable "source" of the Moses story, it is necessary to re-emphasise that in essence and character as well as in content and form, they are completely different from each other. [*See Note* 22, *p.* 221.] In the case of Sargon, his mother, in contrast to the mother of Moses, exposed the child to drowning because it was a bastard! Moreover there is a notable difference in language and local colour. In the case of Sargon everything is Babylonian: The ark is the basket-shaped boat *kuppu*; the material is derived from the Babylonian reed *suri* and was pitched with the asphalt *iddu* commonly used in Babylonia. In the case of Moses there is no trace of these things. Here everything is Egyptian: *tēbā* "the ark" is in meaning and form Egyptian, and the material is of the Egyptian papyrus reed *gōme*=*kema* (Papyrus Nilotica). Thus it is not, as is frequently asserted, the similarity of the two stories that is striking, but actually their dissimilarity.

Another feature that is typical of Egypt deserves mentioning. According to Plutarch (De Iside XVIII), the Egyptian boatmen were especially fond of using the papyrus reed for their boats. They believed that it afforded protection against crocodiles, since Isis had journeyed in a papyrus boat in the search for the remains of Osiris in the Nile. This popular conception may also have had some influence on the choice of the papyrus reed for the ark, a detail which would admirably fit into the Egyptian background.

Granaries Upper part. house vaults
for storing grain. Lower part. sacks of
grain carried to the granary. The
grain was poured into the upper
windows and taken out from the
doors at the bottom.

CHAPTER II

THE BONDAGE

THE Exodus narrative begins with the account of the
Bondage, giving an ample and comprehensive idea of
the Sojourn of Israel in Egypt. As shown above (p. xxxii)
the Hebrews spent a long time in Egypt as a separate,
self-contained entity in the midst of an Egyptian surrounding.

THE HEBREW SETTLEMENTS.—The Hebrews were, however, not the only foreign tribe to settle in the Delta.
We know of other Asiatic tribes who lived in Egypt in
the frontier districts, and who were tolerated by the
Egyptians. This was in conformity with the Egyptian
conception of their racial superiority and their re-

luctance to absorb alien elements. There were of course rare exceptions as in the case of Joseph and some other foreigners who were admitted to high positions. As a whole, however, they were regarded as foreign peoples and so were the Hebrews treated by the Egyptians during their sojourn among them. This attitude is evident from all the narrator has to tell about the relations between Egyptians and Hebrews; and just as the Egyptians abstained from feeding with the Hebrews (Gen. 43^{32}), so the Hebrews preserved their own language, their habits, worship and cult, which was an abomination to the Egyptians (Ex. 8^{26}). But in spite of all this, the Hebrews, as throughout their history among all peoples in all countries, so also in Egypt, assimilated themselves to the foreign environment, adopting Egyptian manners in all walks of life and absorbing Egyptian conceptions in their thought and talk.

From the start indeed, we are shown such an environment as can only be conceived in Egypt: all the arrangements, all the institutions, the officials, and titles, the customs and usages have a peculiar Egyptian character; the whole phraseology and style of narration bears a typical Egyptian stamp.

"GOING UP" FROM EGYPT.—Right at the beginning (Exod. 1 $^{8-10}$) we are told that a new king in Egypt arose, who knew not Joseph and that he decided to oppress the Hebrews who had become strong and numerous, out of fear that in the event of war they would join the enemy and fight against Egypt. The

Hebrew text proceeds here literally "and they will go up from the land." The great historical significance which lies in this expression becomes clear when it is realised that "going up from the land" is the usual Egyptian expression for going to Canaan; for Canaan is a land of mountains and the Egyptian *went up* to that country. This is in full accordance with the expression used in Hebrew several times (e.g., Gen. 50$^{5-9}$), when speaking of going from Egypt to Canaan, whilst in speaking of going from Canaan to Egypt it is said that "they *went down* to Egypt" (Gen. 12^{10}, 42^3, etc.).

The whole passage and the motivation of the oppression can only be understood in the light of the events during the New Kingdom, after the expulsion of the Hyksos from Egypt, more especially in the time of Thutmosis I and Thutmosis III (1536—1447 B.C.). It could only have been written by someone who was exactly informed of the political situation in Egypt and its connections with Canaan and the neighbouring countries, and knew that the Egyptians were afraid that the Hebrews would look for an opportunity of conquering Canaan.

MAKING BRICKS FOR THE PHARAOH.—According to Ex. 1^{14} the Hebrews were forced to make bricks for Pharaoh, when they built the Store-cities Pithom and Raamses for him. The excavations in Egypt actually led to the discovery of Pithom by Edouard Naville, and the fact that many granaries were found there corroborates the Biblical statement. Their remains show that they were actually built with bricks as it is said in the Exodus story.

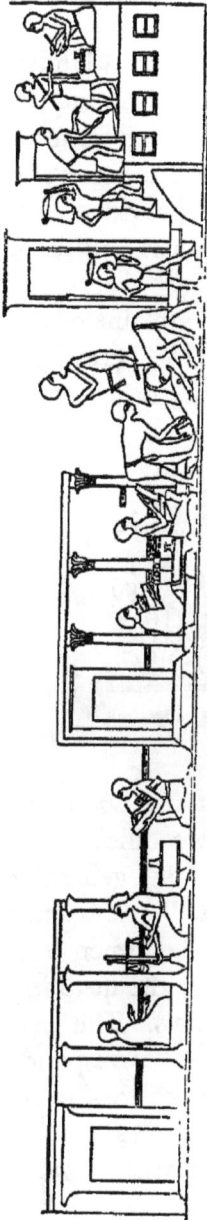

It is curious that some scientific extremists lose their temper to such an extent that they build up a whole polemic on a question which does not exist. Thus an enthusiastic defender of the Bible, who discovered some bricks without straw in the remains of Pithom, hastened to affirm that they were the very same bricks made by the Israelites, as it is said in Exodus 5⁷ that Pharaoh refused to give them straw for bricks. On the other hand, the Egyptologist Eric Peet, in his stubborn disbelief of the Exodus story, used other arguments to prove that they were not made by the Israelites, and that the narrator was extremely ignorant of Egyptian brick manufacture. But both scholars missed the point, because it is said here, and three times more, that Pharaoh refused to give them the straw but ordered that they should supply it themselves. Thus they did not make bricks without straw at all! But the most amazing thing is that Peet went so far as to say that the Egyptians did not use straw at all for making bricks, thus enhancing his view of the utter ignorance of the Biblical author. Unfortunately not only were bricks with straw found in Egypt, but there is also documentary evidence from an Egyptian papyrus in which a man who had to supervise or to construct a building says: "I am not provided with anything; there are no men for making bricks and there is no straw in the district."

This offers a striking parallel to the complaint of the Hebrew supervisors to Pharaoh Ex. 5¹⁶: "There is no straw given unto thy servant, and they say to us, make bricks."

Scribes (*shōterīm*) and taskmasters, or drivers (*nōgesīm*)
with stick in hand.

In connection with the supervising of the bondmen by taskmasters, overseers and scribes, two officials are mentioned *Nōgesīm* and *shōterīm* (Ex. 5¹³⁻¹⁴) generally translated by "taskmasters" and "officers." It is only from the Egyptian picture showing the bondmen and their overseers at work, that we can detect the meaning and function of these two kinds of officials. The first means "drivers, oppressors"—and this corresponds exactly to the Egyptian title *rud.w* employed for "overseers," who supervised the workmen, oppressed and flogged them to their heart's desire. The second word

75

shōterīm does not mean "officers" but is derived from *shatar* "writing" and means "scribes," who, as a matter of fact, had entire control of the bondmen, of their work, of their food and of all other particulars concerning them. In our case they had actually control also over the supply of bricks as it is said in Ex. 5^{6-14} etc.

MEASURING THE BRICKS.—There are scenes depicted on the walls of the tombs which offer the best illustration for many details given in connection with the bondage of Israel in Egypt. On one of the tomb pictures of brick manufacturing, a man is seen crouching before rows of bricks and measuring them, so that the daily quantity prescribed should be supplied by the bondmen. On the opposite corner, a scribe is engaged in registering the supply of bricks, and next to him a man is sitting, stick in hand, to exercise his authority as taskmaster.

How well our author knew what he was talking about can be shown by the expression *mathkōneth* (Ex. 5^8) translated "the tale of the bricks," but which literally means "the measuring of the bricks." He does not say *mispar* the "number," but "the measuring of the bricks," and this is exactly in conformity with what we see. The practical Egyptian did not *count* the bricks, but laid them in rows and *measured* them, just to calculate the space they would fill in a building.

Another relief gives an idea of how the supervisors, who failed to pay the imposed taxes, were handled by the drivers and oppressors, exactly as the Hebrew overseers and scribes were treated by the Egyptian task-masters (Ex. 5^{14}).

All these pictures reproduce so truly and so exactly all the statements given by the narrator of the Bondage, that one could be tempted to think that they have been specially made to illustrate the Bondage story, and it is only astonishing that such critics as Eduard Meyer and Spiegelberg have not suggested that the narrator used these very tomb reliefs in order to invent the legend of Israel's bondage in Egypt.

PHARAOH'S GREAT ANGER.—When Moses appeared before Pharaoh and demanded that the children of Israel should be allowed to go into the wilderness in order to sacrifice to their God, Pharaoh flew into a rage and ordered that heavier tasks should be laid on the Israelites saying (Ex. 5⁸): because they are idle, therefore they cry saying, "Let us go and sacrifice to our God." This he repeated again to the scribes, Exodus 5¹⁷, "Ye are idle, ye are idle: therefore ye say, Let us go and do sacrifice to the Lord."

Now such a reproach, though quite natural and having nothing striking or strange about it so as to make any explanation necessary, yet takes on quite a different complexion when it is seen in the light of Egyptian conditions. On a chalk tablet in the British Museum there are the entries of a labour overseer, in which he recorded daily the number of absent workmen. In most cases the cause is given as illness, also the illness of the wife or the daughter; in one case it is stated the workman had been stung by a scorpion. Many workmen took their duties so little seriously that they stayed away from work for several days. In this case two causes are furnished which give Pharaoh's reproach its local colour. Namely, it is stated that some workmen were idle or that they were pious and remained away from work because they wanted to sacrifice to the gods. Thus we see that next to laziness and piety the sacrificing to the gods is mentioned as an excuse. It seems that the workmen made full use of this pretext. For in a land where rituals and sacrificial cult played so prominent a part, a workman would hardly have been refused time off to sacrifice to the gods or to the dead.

When, then, Moses came to Pharaoh with the demand that the children of Israel should be granted leave for sacrificing to their god, Pharaoh saw therein nothing else but the accustomed pretext and bluntly refused the demand. We now understand why the reason given to Moses so much enraged Pharaoh; for he had had enough with the pious pretensions of his own folk, and it would be too much to allow also the aliens to make use of such pretexts.

STRIKES IN ANCIENT EGYPT.—From the conversation between Pharaoh and Moses another feature emerges, which throws an interesting sidelight on labour conditions in Pharaonic times. When Moses and Aaron asked Pharaoh to give the Hebrews leave for three days to sacrifice to the Lord, Pharaoh said to them (Ex. 5⁴): "Wherefore do ye disturb the people at their labours?" One might properly wonder how it was ever possible in a land of forced labour for Moses and Aaron to disturb the labourers at their work. This difficulty, however, disappears when we learn that also in the land of Pharaoh there were strikes and strike organisers. Such a strike is known to us from the time of Rameses XI in the twelfth century B.C. It was in the royal tombs of Thebes, in the "City of the Dead" as the Egyptians called it. Here a whole group of workers went on strike because the allotted food rations were not regularly forthcoming and some of the sacks of grain found their way into the barns of the officials. The strike continued until the court induced the chief "scribe" of the vizier to satisfy the workers' demands. But even this act of justice was not carried through without a neat bakshish to the fanbearer of the vizier, consisting of two sacks of grain and some writing material, duly recorded by the labour leader in his diary. [*See Note* 23, *p.* 221.]

It now appears clearly that in our case Moses and Aaron were charged by Pharaoh with organising a strike among the Hebrew workers, which must have been a possibility at that time, since otherwise Pharaoh would have employed other means than merely strong language. From such details we can see how exactly the narrator knew the conditions of the country, and so described them as could only one who himself lived in Egypt and was an eyewitness of all these events.

CHAPTER III

THE PLAGUES

TYPICAL EGYPTIAN FEATURES

No one will expect me to discuss whether the ten plagues actually occurred, nor do I propose even to attempt, as many do, to interpret them from a rationalistic point of view as natural phenomena embellished by the author of the Exodus so as to be taken as miracles. We are concerned solely with considering whether the manner in which the plagues are described is characteristic of Egypt, and whether the ideas associated with them by the author are in agreement with Egyptian conditions. If they are typically Egyptian and *could*, if they would, *only* occur in Egypt, then the narrative can only have been written by someone who was familiar with Egyptian conditions, and in a time when such conditions were perfectly known to his readers.

Suppose we had to detect the country or environment in which the author of Matthew, for instance, lived. It would surely not matter whether the episodes related therein actually occurred or not, but only whether it might be possible from the description of these episodes to find out in what country such episodes could be conceived in the manner in which they are described. As soon as it were established that this

The Diary of a taskmaster (see p 77 *seq*)

Growing flax with "goblet-flowers" on the top (see p 91)

The head of the mummy of Thutmosis III (1501–1447 B C), one of
the Pharaohs of the oppression (see
p 73)

Amenophis II (1448-1413 B C), the
Pharaoh of the Exodus (see p 124).

country could be only the Holy Land, then it would be absurd to dispute that Matthew had been written there by a man who was fully conversant with the customs and thoughts of that country and to take the opposite view that it has been written in another country by someone who had drawn his knowledge from second-hand sources—and this only because such a hypothesis would better fit with presupposed ideas and tendencies. To make it still clearer: suppose we read of a king who was threatened that all the football and cricket players of the land would be struck with paralysis just at the start of the game. The first thing we should endeavour to find is the country in which such games are customary and then proceed to ascertain in which language the expressions "football" and "cricket" are used. Once it is established that the country in which such games are best known is Britain, and that such expressions can only be derived from English, then no scientific method in the world, even though most strongly supported by plausible or even fascinating hypotheses could maintain that this story originated in Siberia or in Arabia.

So much for the question of the story concerning the ten plagues as a whole; and now a few observations with regard to the plagues themselves.

Much has already been written about them, and many authors have shown how typically Egyptian some details given about these plagues are, and how even the order in which they are supposed to have succeeded each other coincides with the seasons of the year in Egypt. [See Note 24, p. 221.]

Though it is difficult to deal with the subject without repeating part of what has been said, yet there is still very much that is new to be said about them, and some conceptions which have been formed in connection with the plagues have to be amplified or modified in the light of Egyptian language and folklore.

It would be easy indeed to show that every detail of the account confirms the astonishing familiarity of the author with Egyptian conditions, and how absurd it is to surmise that the author could have written this story far away from Egypt and not from first-hand knowledge But the following examples may suffice.

WHEAT AND SPELT UNDER THE HAIL.—One of the plagues which most impressed Pharaoh is that of the hail. This is only conceivable in a country like Egypt where rain and especially hail are practically unknown; and when it happens, it is looked upon as a supernatural phenomenon of most catastrophic consequences.

In Palestine where it is supposed by the critics to have been written, torrential rains are very frequent and even anxiously awaited, being greeted as the greatest boon, and hailstorms, thunder and lightning are so common that it would be inconceivable that such a plague could have shaken Pharaoh's confidence and broken his stubbornness to such an extent as to make him clamour for relief and surrender abjectly. Had the author lived in Palestine, then he would rather have chosen drought. But what makes the whole story so typically Egyptian is the fact that hailstorms in Egypt do far more damage than in Palestine.

How thoroughly the narrator was acquainted with Egyptian conditions, appears from the following detail: It has already been pointed out that the order of the plagues accorded with the seasons of the year; therefore, that of the hail, being the seventh, may be supposed to have taken place at the beginning of the winter season, say about January. Now we are told (Exodus 9^{31-2}) that the flax and the barley were smitten; "for the barley was in the ear, and the flax was bolled," as it is generally understood. "But the wheat and the spelt were not smitten: for they were not grown up." This fully coincides with the conditions of cereal growth in Egypt, where barley and flax ripen much earlier than wheat; and when the barley and flax are fully grown, the wheat is still young and not so much exposed to damage by hailstones.

There is another striking point which lends additional evidence to the author's knowledge of rural conditions in Egypt. Among the several kinds of grain preserved in the tombs, spelt was also found and it has been established by botanists that spelt was cultivated in Egypt as early as the fourth millennium B.C. Now it would be very astonishing that an author living in Palestine many centuries after the Exodus, and being utterly ignorant of Egyptian conditions, should have known that several centuries before him spelt was known in Egypt. As we shall presently see also the expression used in Hebrew for "bolled" has been misunderstood, and that it can only be explained from Egyptian. [*See Note* 25, *p.* 221.]

THE EGYPTIAN DARKNESS.—In Exodus 10^{22-3} we read of the darkness that it was so thick in all the land of

Egypt that it could be felt. We are further told that the darkness lasted three days and the text proceeds literally: "they saw not one another's face, neither rose any from his place for three days." As for the phenomenon of the darkness itself, it has been already described by many writers. They think of the hot wind, the *hamasin*, which produces a thick dust, filling the whole atmosphere with darkness. In a country like Egypt, where the sun is so brilliant, it is indeed felt as a thick darkness. But what has puzzled modern Biblical critics, is the phrase: "and they saw not one another's face *for three days.*" The whole thing was declared to be a fantastic exaggeration on the part of the author ignorant of Egyptian conditions. But in the "myth of the god kings" which is as old as Egypt itself it is said that the world was filled with darkness and the text proceeds literally "and no one of the men and the gods could see the face of the other *eight days.*" Here we have exactly the same phrase as in our passage, showing that this fantastic exaggeration was first made by a genuine Egyptian writer many centuries before the sojourn of Israel in Egypt, with the difference, that the Hebrew author was less fantastic and excessive than his Egyptian predecessor and therefore reduced the eight days to only three.

THE FIRSTBORN.—And now to another instance: The last and most appalling plague which was represented to be the worst of all was the death of the firstborn. It appears somehow strange that only the firstborn were singled out by the plague, as one might suppose it would have been much more effective in its consequences if it applied to all children. But this becomes quite clear, once we know the position of the firstborn and their prerogative rights and privileges according to Egyptian hierarchical conceptions. Primogeniture was in no other country of such great significance as in court life in Egypt, and in no other hierarchy did the firstborn of the king have such privileges as in Egypt. Here the firstborn, the crown prince, had like the king himself divine rank. He was like his father of divine substance and, as the hierarchical formula puts it "came forth out of the body of the god." As soon as he succeeded to the throne, he was appointed by the gods in person as the heir of Horus, the god king, and was given the title of "*Sa-Ra-en-Khetef*" that is "the son of Ra from his body." From that moment everything in him was divine, he was a god himself. Now the plague was essentially directed against the firstborn of the king, not so much to deprive the monarch of his successor, but to defy the mighty gods of Egypt, to expose their impotence to protect the offspring of the "son of Ra." But it is obvious that if only the firstborn of the king were hit by the plague, it would have been attributed to an accident that could happen at any time, and to any son of the king. In order to make it absolutely certain that it was intended to hit the firstborn of the king himself as the son of the god, the plague was directed against all the firstborn in the whole of Egypt, so that everybody should be convinced that it was the firstborn of the king who was aimed at as the victim. In order to make it still more evident, even the firstborn of beasts were to be included among the victims.

85

Of course this may have had also another meaning, and that is to hit the sacred animals like the Apis bulls worshipped by Egyptians, and the sacred cattle in the precincts of the temples.

It becomes obvious that only one who was very intimately acquainted with the hierarchical ideas prevailing at the court of Pharaoh could have conceived the far-reaching consequences of such a measure. But it would be difficult to understand that an author living remote from those circles and being ignorant of these conditions could even have invented such an incident.

THE FINGER OF GOD.—When Moses inflicted the third plague on the Egyptians (Ex. 8$^{17-18}$) the magicians of Pharaoh were not able to reproduce it as they had done with the previous plagues (Ex. 7^{12}, ^{22}; 8^7). In order to justify their ineptitude they declared that it was "the finger of God" (Ex. 8^{19}). The fact that this expression is said to have come from the mouth of the magicians, and further that such an explanation was considered to be fully sufficient to excuse the failure of their efforts, suggests an Egyptian origin of the expression itself, as well as of the whole idea connected with it.

As a matter of fact "the finger of Seth" was current in magical texts. The "finger of Seth" must have its origin in the myth of his fight against Horus for world domination, and relate to the episode when Seth damaged his eye. The "finger of Seth" was indeed from old a source of terror and threat, especially for the dead, who were exposed to all the vicissitudes suffered by Osiris and Horus at the hands of Seth, so much so that special spell formulae had to be applied in order to avert from them a similar danger from the persecutions of Seth and other gods or demons. The idea of "the finger of God" as very dangerous appears also in connection with Thoth, "the finger of Thoth" (*deba en Dhuty*) being mentioned as a constant threat to Apophis, the monstrous serpent-dragon of the night, and most terrible foe of the sun god Ra.

It is now clear that the plague of lice appeared to the despaired magicians as a blow coming from an unknown source, over which they had no power either to produce or to avert, and thus could only be caused by "the finger of a god" like that of Seth or of another hostile deity. It is, however, very possible that in this connection the magicians did not refer to one of their own gods, but to the God of Moses, recognising that the mysterious power of "the finger of God" was beyond their grasp. At any rate, the expression "finger of God" as well as the whole idea of an atrocious visitation being caused by the "finger of God" are undoubtedly Egyptian.

It is to be noted that even the Hebrew word *ezba* for finger is the same as the Egyptian *deba* so that the identity of both phrases *ezba Elohim* and *deba en neter* in Hebrew and Egyptian for "finger of God" is beyond doubt. Although *deba* may be a Semitic loan word in Egyptian from very old times, the phrase itself is typically Egyptian, and was in use as far back as the Pyramid texts more than a thousand years before the sojourn of Israel in Egypt.

THE MAIDSERVANT BEHIND THE MILL.—In Exodus 11[5] we read: "and all the firstborn in the land of Egypt

Maidservants grinding and kneading.

shall die, from the firstborn of Pharaoh that sitteth upon his throne, even unto the firstborn of the maidservant that is behind the mill." Here the "maidservant behind the mill" is a phrase which I have been unable to trace in any other Semitic language, but is genuinely Egyptian and denotes the lowest social grade. To grind the grain for the needs of the household was the lowest occupation an Egyptian woman had to undertake, and was reserved either for destitute women or for prisoners undergoing penal servitude. The contrast between "the firstborn of Pharaoh who sits on his throne" and the firstborn of "the maidservant behind the mill" becomes now very graphic and appears extremely humiliating for the Pharaoh who prided himself of being the son of Ra (*Sa-Ra*). It must have sounded in his ears as a phrase like "from the firstborn who sits on the throne at Buckingham Palace to the firstborn of the charwoman of Seven Dials" would sound to us.

THE GIRDLES ON THE LOINS.—There are other little touches in the Exodus narrative which do not attract

the special attention of the reader and yet are typical
Egyptian features which indicate the adaptation of
Egyptian customs by the Hebrews and the author's
familiarity with intimate Egyptian life. In Ex. 12[11]
the order is given to the children of Israel to eat the
Paschal lamb with their loins girded, with their
shoes on their feet, and their staff in their hand, that
they should eat it in haste. As it was expected that
Pharaoh would hasten to drive them out of the country,
they should be prepared to leave at any moment.
Had the narrator lived in the land of Israel many
centuries after the Exodus, he would have told them
to hasten with the meal with cloaks (*simlāh*) on their
shoulders to leave hurriedly, because this is the way
in which a Hebrew would set out for a journey in his
own country. But the Egyptian when going out had a
girdle around his loins, his sandals on, and a stick
in his hand. Thus the author had an Egyptian environment in mind and his order to be prepared to
leave at any moment sounds as if we would say: have
your hat and coat on, ready to leave. [*See Note* 26, *p.* 221.]

Notables and priests having girdles on the loins and
walking sticks in hand, some of them having the name of
the owner written on them.

89

.

CHAPTER IV

Typical Egyptian Expressions and Phrases

IN addition to all these details which confirm the familiarity of the author with Egyptian conditions, there is strong linguistic evidence to prove that certain expressions used in connection with the plagues also are so much in keeping with the spirit of the Egyptian language that they can only be understood as renderings of Egyptian words. Moreover, the spirit of the Egyptian language is not only revealed in single words but in some cases also in whole phrases which are so typically Egyptian that no one but a Hebrew, who was writing under the influence of Egyptian, could adapt them to the Hebrew language.

THE VOICES OF GOD.—One of the most remarkable instances is given in the use of the "voices of Elohim" for thunder. The Hebrew text in Exodus 9^{23} has for thunder *qōlōth* "voices" and 9^{28} "voices of God" for "mighty thunders." This is not the usual expression for thunder in Hebrew but is the common designation among Egyptians for thunder. For them it was *kheru en neter*, "a voice of God" or *kheru en beya*, "a voice of heaven," or the voice of Amon in heaven, exactly as it is called in Ex. 9^{28}, "the voice of Elohim."

90

THE "GOBLETS" OF FLAX.—Another instance is provided by the use of *gib'ōl* for "bolled," Ex. 9³¹. It is the more instructive as it can only be understood from close observation of the growth of flax and only have been coined by someone who had the appearance and shape of the bud before his eyes. The explanation of *gib'ol* was in vain sought from Hebrew or from roots of kindred Semitic languages. This failure was due to the fact that etymologists are accustomed to draw their knowledge from dictionaries, comparing sound with sound, letter with letter, root with root, making all kinds of combinations, but seldom think of deserting the sacred precincts of their studies to look at nature and to observe the things themselves which are far more enlightening than the dead letters of grammars and dictionaries. Now if we go out into the field of flax when it is fully ripe, we shall observe that it has flowers which look like little cups. As a cup is called in Hebrew "*gabī'a*" and *gib'ōl* has been coined with regard to the shape of the flower looking like "a little cup," here, too, it is difficult to imagine that an author living in a country far away from Egypt, where he could hardly see any flax growing, could have created such a word in Hebrew which most beautifully conveys the shape of the flax flower. [*See Note* 27, *p.* 222.]

THE MIRRORS OF THE HEBREW WOMEN.—A similar case in which the traditional explanation of a Hebrew word is confirmed by Egyptian archaeology, is the following. In Ex. 38⁸ it is said that the laver of brass was made of the looking-glasses which the women brought to the Tabernacle.

Now brass mirrors were known long ago from Roman and Etruscan times, but not from Egypt at such an early age as the Egyptian period of Israel. But the excavations have brought to light an exceedingly great number of brass mirrors from earliest times, and of specially exquisite make from the New Kingdom, the very period of Israel's sojourn in Egypt.

An Egyptian lady holding a mirror of brass like those of the Hebrew women

From one tomb relief we can see that the ladies of Ancient Egypt knew perfectly, as do the modern girls, the art of rouging their lips before the looking-glass.

In addition to that it may be stated that it was a technical speciality of Egyptian craftsmanship to make larger brass vessels, magnificently polished on the outside in the same manner as mirrors were polished. Thus the statement that the laver was made of the mirrors conveys at the same time the idea that it was cast and polished with the same technique as the mirrors. This is a very important detail, because it shows how very well acquainted the author was with Egyptian craftsmanship of that time when the Hebrews were still living in close contact with the Egyptians; and thus we have here a further instance of the exactness of the Exodus tradition. To this archæological confirmation the linguistic evidence is to be added, as the Hebrew word for mirror is *mar'ōth*, which literally means "showing objects" fully accords with the Egyptian expression *maa* "mirrors" also formed from *maa* "seeing and showing", so that the Hebrew is a literal rendering of the Egyptian word. [*See Note* 28, *p.* 222.]

It is necessary to emphasise all these details, because, if we turn to the Biblical critics for enlightenment we shall find that that portion of Exodus is attributed by them to a writer of the sixth century B.C., i.e., eight centuries after the Exodus, because they cannot believe that the Hebrews had knowledge of brass mirrors at such an early time. Wellhausen, the father of modern Biblical criticism, went so far as to ask us to believe that the details of the mirrors is altogether a late interpolation of a legendary character.

THE EYE OF THE EARTH.—The following example is not only illuminating for the use the author made of metaphorical expressions which can only have been known to someone who was acquainted with the Egyptian sacred books, but is also characteristic for the manner in which he divested them from their original mythological conception. Ex. 10^{4-5} reads: "tomorrow will I bring the locusts into thy coast: and they shall cover the face of the earth, that one cannot be able to see the earth."

For "the face of the earth" the Hebrew original has "the eye of the earth," a much-debated phrase which has been interpreted in many ways, by far-fetched hypothesis, without arriving at any satisfactory meaning. The explanation is, however, very simple indeed.

The Egyptians conceived the sun as one eye and the moon as the other eye of Ra, the first being open by day and the second by night. Now the monotheistic author would not possibly call the sun "eye of Ra," because he did not believe in Ra or that the sun was his eye; he therefore substituted it by the metaphorical expression "eye of the earth," which conveys the same idea. [*See Note* 29, *p.* 222.]

That "the eye of the earth" refers to the sun is best shown by Ex. 10[5] where it is said that the locusts "covered the eye of the whole earth so that the earth was darkened"; this can only mean that the locusts flew up in such dense swarms that they obscured the sunshine as with a thick cloud. By the "covering the eye of the earth" reference is made to the extraordinarily terrifying, immeasurably large size of the locust swarms which darkened the light of the sun. This phenomenon has frequently been observed, and related on several occasions by trustworthy eyewitnesses, as for instance in describing the great plague of locusts in 1916 in Palestine. There the darkening of the light of the sun by swarms of locusts was the most prominent feature, as was emphasised in several newspapers and scientific periodicals in almost identical language. The same phenomenon recently occurred (23 July, 1931) in

Angola, when swarms of locusts were so dense that, according to reports, they *"completely obscured the sun for some hours."*

As it happens with many metaphors the use of "eye of the earth" was extended from the object to its effect, and in this case from the sun to the light spread by it over the earth, so that "the eye of the earth" was applied not only to the disc itself, but to the light covering the earth. So we find that Num. 22[5] in describing the panic of the Moabites at the appearance of the Hebrews, applies the same metaphor to their great numbers that "covered the eye of the earth," meaning that there was not a spot left which they had not occupied.

MOSES AS "GOD" AND AARON AS HIS "MOUTH."—Ex. 4[16] reads literally: "he (Aaron) shall be to thee a mouth and thou shalt be to him a god (*Elohim*)." Here "mouth" is used metaphorically for representative, being a literal rendering of the Egyptian *ra* "mouth," a very common title of a high office at the court of Pharoah. The office of a "mouth" was so important indeed that it was held by the highest state dignitaries. Thus especially in the New Kingdom the titles "mouth" (*ra*) and "chief mouth" (*ra-hery*) frequently occur in reference to persons of high rank who, as chief superintendents and overseers of public works, acted as intermediaries between the king and government officials. In some cases they are called "mouth" or "chief mouth of the king," e.g., Ahmose, the commander-in-chief of Thutmosis III, says of himself: "(I was) the mouth of the king who brought tranquillity to the whole land and who filled the heart of the king with love and satisfaction every day" and "(the king) made me chief mouth of his house."

As a rule it was the heir to the throne who occupied the position of a "chief-mouth" to the king, thus, e.g., Haremheb was, as crown prince, the "chief mouth" to the king; Rameses II when ten years old received the title "chief mouth of the army" as commander-in-chief, and Rameses III when still crown prince was called "great chief mouth for the land of Egypt." The "mouth" or "chief mouth" was in many cases the most confidential and exalted position at court, ranking immediately after the king.

In the light of this explanation it now becomes clear, what is meant by placing Moses as a god (*Elohim*) over Aaron. As "mouth" is identical with the Egyptian title for representative and deputy of the king, "god" (*Elohim*) must obviously refer to the authority immediately above the "mouth" and subsequently only Pharaoh could be meant. This is actually the case: Elohim is used here not in the Hebrew sense of God but is a faithful rendering of the Egyptian title *neter* "god" which was one of the attributes of Pharaoh. It was applied to the living as well as to the dead Pharaoh, thus, e.g., "the glorious god," or "the god without equal." In many cases the Pharaoh is also described as "the good god" (*neter nefer*) or "the great god" (*neter aa*). In our passage Elohim is thus a substitute of Pharaoh, conveying with a certain ironical glance at Pharaoh's pretensions, that Moses was to be the Pharaoh over Aaron, who in his turn would be his "mouth," i.e., his deputy.

But it is not only in relation to Aaron that Moses is to appear as *neter*, but even before Pharaoh who claims to be himself a god, Moses alone is to be the *neter* for the purpose of making known to Pharaoh the superior power of Jehovah. This is the real meaning of Ex. 7[1], where the same expression Elohim is again used in the Egyptian sense of *ntr*: "See, I have made thee a god (*Elohim*) to Pharaoh." The whole is conceived throughout in an Egyptian spirit, and was intended for people thoroughly familiar with the conditions and the language of Egypt, so that they would immediately recognize in the Hebrew "mouth" and "god" (*Elohim*) subsequently, the Egyptian *ra* and *neter*, and understand that Moses was meant to be the *neter*=god, i.e., the supreme chief, and Aaron his *ra*="mouth."

"IN THOSE NUMEROUS DAYS."—Another phrase which deserves to be considered here, is Ex. 2[23], "and it came to pass *in process of time*, that the king of Egypt died." In "process of time" is a paraphrase of the Hebrew text which literally reads, "in those numerous days." This was interpreted as meaning a long period after the foregoing events. It was hence concluded by some Biblical critics that it had to be attributed to a source different from that of the previous text. The strange wording of this phrase caused much speculative interpretation and it was also suggested that Ex. 4[19], where Moses was told to return to Egypt because all the men who sought his life were dead, could not possibly be connected with this passage. In reality "after numerous days" is only a mode of speech very frequent in Egyptian literature, especially in the popular narrative style, in tales and stories like the Exodus account. It is an almost colourless formula and had long since lost its literal meaning. This is so much the case, that it is repeated several times at the beginning of different sections in one and the same story, just to mark the advance in the sequence of the chief events, without implying any lapse of a long period between the various phases of the narrative. Thus the well-known story of the Two Brothers, written in the thirteenth century B.C., almost every new paragraph begins with the same phrase, "and after numerous days thereafter," although the events related followed on one another and comprised only very short periods, and in one case the "numerous days" hardly cover the time of a few months extending over the pregnancy of the princess referred to in the story. This and similar phrases, as, for instance, "and thereafter when days have gone," or "in one of those days it happened that and that" are to be found in other stories which belong to a much earlier period, as, for instance, in the stories of King Cheops in *Pap. Westcar* of the Hyksos time.

This example clearly shows that our narrator, in adopting this Egyptian phrase, did not mean to convey that a very considerable time elapsed from the foregoing events, but, on the contrary, used it with the purpose of introducing successive events of one and the same story. Hence far from marking a distant period derived from a different source, the Egyptian colouring of the phrase makes it obvious that it belongs to the same story. By adding that this phrase is most typical of the literature of the New Kingdom, in the period of Israel's sojourn in Egypt, the close connection between the Hebrew phrase and its Egyptian pattern becomes more evident, and furnishes another unmistakable proof in favour of our view, that the Exodus narrative was composed in the Exodus period. But the most important point is the impossibility of denying that Ex. 4[19] cannot but refer to the death of the king of Egypt, Ex. 2[23]. Here, as in the story of the Two Brothers, the interval between the two events covered only a short period, probably a few years, as the son born to Moses in Midian must still have been a baby, when returning to Egypt (Ex. 4[25]).

By establishing the true meaning of this phrase all the conjectures, both of a historical and textual critical character, made in connection with Ex. 2[23], fall to the ground, and we thereby realise how shaky the foundations are, on which some of the very far-reaching hypotheses about the various "sources" of the Pentateuch are based, and how quickly and hopelessly they are shattered by the evidence from Egyptian.

"SINCE THE FOUNDATION OF THE KINGDOM OF EGYPT."— In the Exodus story there are phrases which at a first glance do not call for any particular attention and the reader passes over them without noting in them anything out of the ordinary. Nevertheless, when seen in the light of Egyptian thought they appear in their true Egyptian colour and reveal the author's perfect knowledge of the hierarchical views the Egyptians had of the

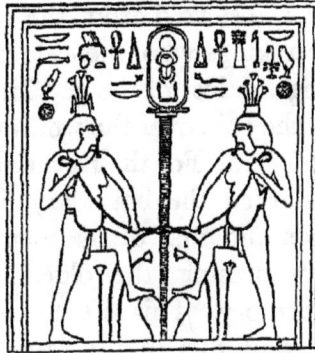

The god of Upper Egypt (left)
and the god of Lower Egypt
(right) tying together the lotus
flower and the papyrus flower
symbolising the unification of
both lands of the South and the
North

earliest developments at the dawn of their history.
Thus, Ex. 9[18] we read that Moses, in announcing the
hail, said unto Pharaoh that it would be "such as hath
not been in Egypt since the day it was founded until
now" and in Ex. 9[24] it is said of the hail: "such as there
was none like it in all the land of Egypt since it became a
nation." The real meaning of this allusion to Egypt
only becomes clear, with full significance, when we
learn that the Egyptians from the earliest times regarded
the foundation of the Kingdom of Upper and Lower
Egypt as the greatest and most significant event in their
history. Although the exact date was not known,
nevertheless the memory thereof reached back to the
remotest period, still remaining vivid as late as the New
Kingdom. It was always conceived as the moment
when Egypt began to exist as a people, when the rule

100

over Egypt was transferred from the gods of primeval days to the man kings who thenceforth became their heirs representing the last of the god king Horus, son of Osiris, to whom the rule over the world was handed over by Ra, the creator-god. For the Egyptians the beginning of that epoch marked the boundary line between the world of the gods and that of the men who descended from them, thus forming the oldest epoch of their history within memory. This is the event to which our passages allude, and this in the same manner as the Egyptians themselves spoke of it. In the first passage we have in the words "in Egypt from the day it was founded" the literal reproduction of an Egyptian phrase to characterise something unusual, unheard of, since the earliest times within human memory; thus Thutmosis III says that Amon rejoiced over him more than over all the kings who have been "in the land since it was founded." Similarly, it is said also of Thutmosis III that Amon "loved his own son so very much more than any king who has been since the primordial time of the land." On another occasion it is said of the new con- struction of a fortress "never had its like been made since the primordial time of the land." A closer parallel to our passage is offered in the well-known hymn to the sun god Aton, by Akhenaton, where it is said that whenever the sun rises it brings forth crops for the King since Aton "founded the land." These examples, to which many more could be added, show how closely our passages follow in wording and spirit the Egyptian manner of speaking. [*See Note* 30, *p.* 222.]

"SINCE EGYPT BECAME A NATION."—In the second passage reference is made to the establishment of the kingdom when Egypt became a people in the same way in which the Egyptians spoke when describing events of an extraordinary nature. Thus, it is said of Rameses II that he brought numerous bags of wonderful genuine malachite, "the like of which had not been made since the kings and the former ones."

How closely *the establishment of* the kingdom and the period of the rule of the god-kings were bound up together in the mind of the Egyptian is shown by the fact that he harked back also to the time of the gods whenever he spoke of something very ancient, or exceptionally unusual, that had never been seen before. The familiar formula was *dzer rek neter* "since the time of the god" meaning either Ra as the first, or Horus as the last, of the god kings on earth whose throne was then occupied by the first man king as the heir to Horus. Thus we are told of a glorious weighing scale of burnished copper, "the like of which had not been made since the time of god" (Thoth).

SINCE THE TIME OF THE GODS.—Similarly we find the court addressing Rameses II: "since the time of the god there has been none like unto thee, neither beheld by face nor heard in words" or that a drought prevailed in the land Akita "since the time of the god." In the wisdom of *Mery-Ka-Ra* it is said of the Asiatic that "since the time of Horus he has been fighting and conquers not." In the Israel stela of Merneptah it is said of Egypt that she is "the only daughter of Ra since the gods."

102

Another typical phrase for the characterisation of an astonishing event as something unique and unheard of, is Ex. 10[14] "before it had never been its like," or 11[6]: "such as there was none like it." This mode of exaggerating was very customary among the Egyptians and occurs again and again in narratives, historical records, and also in poetic texts alluding to primeval times in the same sense as in the cited passages above. With particular fervour the Egyptian gives the assurance on every occasion, as already noted, that the like had never been seen, never been made or never been heard "since the time of the god", or "the gods", or "since the primordial time of the land," or "since the former ones," or "the forefathers." Especially favoured are such phrases in the boastful, pompous reports of the kings or great dignitaries vaunting their valiant deeds, the grandeur of their buildings and splendour of their gifts to temples and gods, as for instance of the votive table dedicated by Thutmosis III to "his father" Amon: "never was the like made in this land since the days of the former ones," or of the fame of Thutmosis I, "the like has not been in the annals of 'the forefathers' since the followers of Horus," i.e., the kings that followed Horus; or "never has the like occurred since the primordial time of the two lands."

THE "EARLIEST DAYS."—All these expressions, especially those relating to primeval times and first beginnings, are in another respect very instructive for the understanding of two other passages alluding to the covenant with the "first ones" (ancestors) Lev. 26[45], and to the "first days" (days that are past) Deut. 4[32], as the Hebrew has it. Here as in Egyptian, great events are described as something which since the first forefathers and the earliest days have never been seen or heard. But with the difference that by the further description of these "earliest days" as "the day when God created man upon earth," the conception of the primeval age is freed from polytheistic and mythological elements, and is defined as the true beginning not of mythical but of the real world in which, through the creation of man the awakening of conscience first became possible. Here we see clearly how Egyptian mythological formulae of dogmatic and hierarchic nature were transplanted to monotheistic soil and thereby endowed with religious and moral force, the like of which never existed in Egypt. Precisely such passages indicate that the altering of the Egyptian phraseology by the Hebrew writer was deliberate for the purpose of adapting Egyptian wording to monotheistic thought.

THE "FOREFATHERS" OF PHARAOH.—Another phrase which escapes our special attention but which assumes a particular significance in the light of Egyptian thought, is Ex. 10⁶. Speaking of the locusts to the Pharaoh Moses said, "and they shall fill thy houses, and the houses of all thy servants, and the houses of all the Egyptians; which neither thy fathers, nor thy fathers' fathers have seen, since the day that they were upon the earth unto this day." In order properly to appreciate the full bearing of this threat launched against Pharaoh, it must be remembered that the Pharaoh always claimed to be the corporal, "son of Ra from his body," and that on every occasion it was said that the great gods Amon, Ra and indeed all the primeval gods were his very own fathers and forefathers. It was, therefore, plain for every Egyptian that, whenever reference was made to the fathers and forefathers of the king, it was intended to convey the idea of his divine parentage, alluding to the "gods that were before him" to "his fathers, all the gods" just as he was called simply "the god," or "the good god." When, therefore, Moses mentioned before Pharaoh in menacing tone his fathers and his fathers' fathers, it denoted not merely an onslaught against the King, but also a blow against the deep-rooted reverence for his ancestors the "gods that were before him." Nothing indeed could have given Pharaoh a greater shock than such arrogant speech from the mouth of a Hebrew who did not believe in his divinity, and still less in the divinity of his dead forefathers, "the gods who rest in their pyramids."

It is very significant to note that all these phrases only occur in the Exodus narrative in connection with the sojourn of Israel in Egypt.

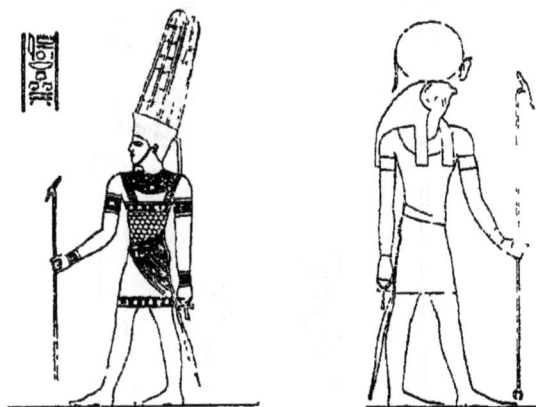

Gods (Amon and Ra) holding rods, or staves.

the hieroglyphic sign of a god-determinative the rod was more clearly characterised as divine. [*See Note* 31, *p.* 222.]

For our purpose it is of importance that rods with heads of gods, or of sacred animals symbolising certain divinities, as, for instance, the cow as Hathor, the ram as Amon, the hawk as Horus, very frequently appear in reliefs and statues of kings, priests and high officials of the eighteenth and nineteenth dynasties, that is in the period of Israel's sojourn in Egypt and of Moses' activities before the Pharaoh.

If to all this we add that in all the cases when such rods are mentioned, the rod is called *med* or *medu*, and that on the other hand for Moses' and Aaron's rod the word *mattēh* is exclusively used, which in spite of all efforts cannot be explained from a Semitic stem, there can hardly be any doubt as to the Egyptian origin of the word *mattēh*. [*See Note* 32, *p.* 222.] The identity is enhanced by the fact that the description of Moses'

107

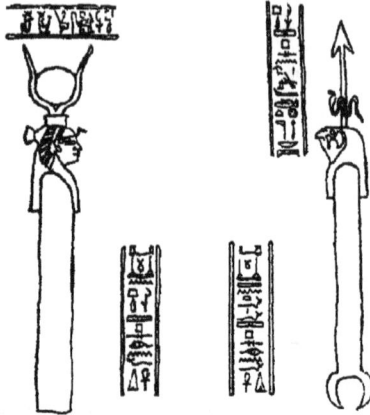

Holy rods with the head of Hathor and
Horus.

rod as "rod of God" (Ex. 4²⁰, 17⁹) literally corresponds
to the Egyptian *medu-neter* "rod of god." Of course
Moses' rod cannot possibly have borne any image in
the fashion of the Egyptian rods because this was
obnoxious to the God of Israel; but it may have been
inscribed with the name of Elohim or Jehovah being
endowed with divine power. It is to be noted that only
after the burning of the bush the rod became a "rod of
God."

THE ROD AND THE CROCODILE.—The Egyptian character of Moses' rod is particularly apparent in the
magical use made of it in the Exodus story. As a matter
of fact it is only the Egyptian environment which
teaches us how to understand the association of the rod
with the serpent Ex. 4²⁻³, and to detect the real nature
of what was done by Aaron with his rod before Pharaoh
and his court, Ex. 7⁹⁻¹². For this purpose it must be

108

pointed out that in Ex. 4³ the Hebrew word for serpent is *nahāsh*, whereas in Ex. 7⁹⁻¹² it is *tannīn*, which does not at all mean serpent as it is generally rendered, and this is done only here, in order to accord it with Ex. 4³, whereas, in all other eleven passages where it occurs, it is conceived as a monster, as a dragon of a mythological character. In reality its true meaning is clearly apparent from Ezek. 29³ and 32², where it is applied to Pharaoh. As we know that Pharaoh was represented as a crocodile, symbolising Egypt's power and might, and that he was deified as the crocodile god Sobek, it is obvious that in applying *tannīn* to Pharaoh it can only mean the crocodile. [*See Note* 33, *p.* 223.] As a matter of fact the whole passage Ezek. 29³⁻⁷ is a very vivid description of the crocodile and some terms are typically Egyptian, especially the two last words of verse three which literally mean, "I made myself," and exactly reproduce the Egyptian conception that Pharaoh, as a divine incarnation, attributed to himself like all the gods, the virtue of self-creation. In accepting this meaning for *tannīn* all other passages become perfectly clear and then we realise that it always refers to the crocodile and nowhere to whale or a mythological monster. [*See Note* 34, *p.* 223.]

From all this it results, that Aaron's rod was converted into a crocodile and not as Moses' rod into a serpent. In the first case when God revealed himself to Moses, the miracle with the serpent was destined to show to Moses and to the Hebrews that the serpent, the holiest symbol of gods and kings as of divine substance, could be produced from a rod. In the case of Aaron, however, it should be brought home to Pharaoh that the mighty crocodile, the terror of the waters, was nothing more than a rod in the hand of Jehovah's envoy. Here it was not even Moses, the direct messenger of God, but his inspired prophet Aaron (Ex. 7¹) who produced the miracle; and when Pharaoh's magicians repeated it, Aaron's superiority was demonstrated by all their crocodiles being swallowed by his rod. The whole scene is so substantially Egyptian that it could not have been conceived or understood in its whole far-reaching consequences but in Egypt.

As to the association of the serpent with the rod there is a picture showing Thoth, the god of writing and the scribe of the gods, holding in his hands a holy rod headed by the hawk which is his symbol, and having a serpent wound round the rod. But there is also a certain parallel to the conversion of the rod into a serpent and a crocodile in the Egyptian myth of the god kings "Shu and Geb," where we find that the serpent *Yaaret* has converted itself into a crocodile in the mythical lake of *Desdes* and become the crocodile-god Sobek.

Thoth with his rod surmounted by the head of a hawk, his symbol, with a serpent twisted round it.

AARON'S ROD.—From the foregoing description of the rod of the gods and the priests, we arrive at a clearer understanding of the whole episode around Aaron's rod (Num. 17²⁻¹¹).

110

The rebellion of Korah and his associates against Moses because of his confining the priesthood to Aaron's family (Num. 16) was only a link in the chain of uprisings called for against Moses by those who advocated the adoption of a hierarchical priesthood with all the privileges and prerogatives. The ambitious striving for priestly powers was the cause of heated disputes even within Aaron's family itself (Lev. 10$^{1-2}$). Now the Levite Korah together with many "princes of the assembly and men of renown" from other tribes, rose to combat the limitation of the priesthood to Aaron's family. They demanded its extension to all members of the community "as all of them were holy, and God was among them" (Num. 16$^{2-3}$), just as it was the case in Egypt, where every prince or high official could become a "priest before the god." In this respect they thought they could impose their claims upon Moses because it was he himself who proclaimed "a kingdom of priesthood" (Ex. 19^6) and the holiness of the whole of Israel (Lev. 19^2). Of course their contention was only a pretext, as the true sense of that proclamation was to oppose the recognition of any individual right to self-arrogated privileges derived from any alleged divine or hierarchical prerogatives. Likewise were "priesthood" and "holiness" to be divested of their ritual meaning, and transferred to a purely religious and ethical ground. But the people were not able to grasp such ideals, and Moses had to yield in spite of overcoming the seditious opposition with resolute force. Nevertheless, he did not go in his concessions beyond his original scheme to limit the priestly rights, establishing Aaron as the only priest

111

and progenitor of all subsequent priest generations for all times.

Now it is evident that Aaron's followers after their experience with the revolt of the golden calf (Ex. 32²⁷ seq.) and that of Aaron's sons (Lev. 10¹⁻²), distrusted Moses and brought great pressure to bear upon him to secure irrevocably their acknowledged rights. On the other hand "the princes of the assembly and the men of renown" could not be satisfied with the issue of Korah's rebellion and the people murmured against Moses and Aaron (Num. 16⁴²). Moses had therefore to discover some way out of the difficulty in order to avoid further dispute on either side, and to keep all parties within their limits. He thus resorted to a solution which reveals his acquaintance with the Egyptian usage of keeping in their temples holy rods inscribed with the names of gods, kings and priests. Only on this assumption it is comprehensible that Moses could have come to the idea of demanding the rods of the princes of Israel in order to inscribe their names on them and to lay them "before the Lord" for the purpose of choosing his priest (17²⁻⁴). After the decision had turned out in Aaron's favour, Moses with the intention of preventing any abuse being made of Aaron's rod, placed it before the ark of the covenant to be kept "for a token against the rebels" (17¹⁰), and surely also to prevent any priest from using the rod for himself, and calling himself "priest of the rod of God" after the fashion of the Egyptian priests with their rods. It seems that also Moses' rod was kept in the tabernacle "before the Lord" close to the ark of the covenant. This appears from Numb. 20⁹, where it is

112

said that Moses took the rod "from before the Lord" in order to smite the rock for water, as it cannot possibly refer to Aaron's but only to Moses' rod. [*See Note* 35, *p.* 223.]

THE ROD AS EMBLEM OF THE TRIBE.—The symbolical significance of the rod as emblem of power and authority furnishes the key to the association of rod with tribe in the use of the same word *mattēh* for rod and tribe, which is not to be found in any Semitic language but Hebrew. As we have just seen from Num. 17² every one of the tribal princes had his rod. It symbolised the autonomy and sovereignty of the tribe and was carried by the chieftain as the attribute of leadership and authority. He received it from the tribe upon his election, in the same way as Pharaoh received his royal insignia from the gods on his accession to the throne. In the course of time one got so much accustomed to speak of "the rod" as representing the tribe that in the long run it became synonymous with tribe, obtaining such currency that it simply was used for "tribe."

The establishing of such extension of meaning from "rod" to "tribe," explains the use of another analogous expression, namely *shēbet*, for "rod, staff" and "tribe." Originally it meant most probably whipping-rod (Is. 10⁵; Proverbs 13²⁴ and 26³). This reminds us of the fact that stick and flail were among the royal insignia of the Pharaoh and it seems that in Gen. 49¹⁰ *shēbet* is actually conceived as such a symbol of the tribal ruler. Here we observe the same process of transferring the meaning from rod to tribe, because here too their identity became

113

so obvious that the same word was used to designate them both. It seems, however, that there is a nuance between *shēbet* and *mattēh* inasmuch as *shēbet* represents a higher degree of authority, as a kind of sceptre, and was therefore applied to the whole tribe, whereas *mattēh* was also applied to a branch of the tribe.

A man carrying baskets of bread on a staff.

THE "STAFF OF BREAD."—Through the connection of *mattēh* with the Egyptian rod, another Biblical phrase is explained. In several passages, thus, Lev. 26[26], Ez. 4[16], 5[16], 14[13] and Psalm 105[16], it is spoken of "breaking the staff of bread." Although nobody doubts that it means famine, still the background for the metaphorical usage of "staff of bread" in this sense is not clear. This is supplied, however, by the custom of carrying bread-baskets on a staff frequently depicted on Egyptian reliefs. Thus when the staff of bread lies broken, there is no bread to be carried and this means starvation. In this light Levit. 26²⁶ is rendered more intelligible where it is said that ten women shall take the bread to one oven. This would happen because the baker's boys would not continue bringing plenty of bread in their baskets carried on the staff into the houses, and the ovens of the bakeries would be out of work for scarcity of bread.

In the course of time the plastic sense of this phrase has faded away and it became metaphorical for famine. The same applies also to the breaking of staff of water, Is. 3¹, which follows on the breaking of the staff of bread, as the water-pails too were carried on staffs between two men. But here the Hebrew word *mish'ān* is used instead of the Egyptian loan word *mattēh*. In the English Bible this passage is paraphrased.

Of course the explanation from the Egyptian reliefs does not mean that the origin of the phrase must be Egyptian. As the same custom of carrying bread, fruit and water-pails on staffs was also common in Canaan (Num. 13²³), the metaphorical use of the phrase can have been at home as well in Canaan as in Egypt. Nevertheless, it is from the Egyptian pictures that we learn the original meaning of the phrase.

·

CHAPTER VI

THE DATE OF THE EXODUS IN THE LIGHT OF NEW EVIDENCE

DISCRIMINATION AGAINST BIBLICAL RECORDS.—As in the case of the Joseph story, the historicity and veracity of the Exodus account are, likewise, treated with distrust by Biblical critics and a few Egyptologists, because they find in it legendary and mythical details, but the historical value is denied by them even to that part which betrays no trace of mythical features. This method is, however, not applied by the same scholars to non-Biblical documents, as it does not occur to them to question the historical validity of such records, even when permeated with mythical details. This discrimination, against the Joseph and Exodus stories, perfectly fits within the attitude pursued by scholars adhering to Biblical criticism when they write the history of Israel, or of the literature of the Bible, but thoroughly differs from true and sound scientific methods of historiography. Unprejudiced writers of ancient history base their views on the documents transmitted by the peoples themselves, and, as a whole, accept ancient records as the essential foundation for historical reconstruction. Even in cases where only myths or legends are available, they attempt to detect at the back of mythological representations the historical

116

kernel and the facts enveloped in legendary wrappings. Only when the Bible is involved do the critics, and their adepts from among Egyptologists and Assyriologists, take their own very hypothetical theories as foundation, and in using adverse arguments, they mainly contribute to discredit the Biblical statements and deprive them of their true meaning. In many cases the critics do not take the Biblical texts in their plain meaning, but construe their statements on arbitrary interpretations and go even further in distorting the texts by introducing alterations which they call corrections and emendations, but which in most cases only reveal an astounding ignorance of the Hebrew language and its spirit. It is in following this path that the whole Exodus narrative is converted into a legend, being denied that trustworthiness granted to other records of antiquity, though in some cases they cannot compare with the Biblical records in precision and soberness.

A very curious stand is taken up by Alan H. Gardiner in following H. R. Hall's theory. In spite of stating that "the details of the Exodus story are mythical," he is prepared to admit the historicity of that part of the story which deals with the sojourn of Israel in Egypt and their departure from Egypt; only he maintains that these events are not to be conceived as referring to the Hebrews, but to the invasion of the Hyksos into and their expulsion from Egypt! They are, in his opinion, to be regarded as reminiscences taken over by a later Hebrew author from the history of the Hyksos, and simply put on to the Hebrews. It results that one part of the Exodus story is to be dismissed as mythical, and the other part, which is not mythical, is to be shifted from the ground of Hebrew history and linked up with the history of the Hyksos, thus rejecting the idea, that a piece of history written in Hebrew by a Hebrew author, can have any documentary value for the history of the Hebrews. [*See Note* 36, *p.* 223.]

This theory, though it may appear very ingenious to people who go hunting for ideas of extreme originality, has admittedly not even the merit of being original. It is only a revival of a confusion introduced by the Egyptian priest Manetho, of the third century B.C., in his ill-famed history of Egypt. In some extracts transmitted to us by Josephus in his book *Against Apion* I §14, we are told that the Hyksos, an abominable people of lepers, oppressed the Egyptians many centuries, and that they were eventually driven out of Egypt, whence they went to Judea and built there the city of Jerusalem. Now the exponents of the Exodus-Hyksos theory seize this obvious confusion of the Hyksos with the Hebrews, as the basis for their contention against the validity of the Biblical narrative as a record of Israel's history.

The most striking feature is the fact that there is not one Egyptologist who would not admit Manetho's utter untrustworthiness and ignorance of the most essential events of Egyptian history. But this attitude does not lack its amusing note: Manetho, because he hated the Hebrews, identified them with the Hyksos whom he stigmatised as lepers; and Josephus, because he loved his people, took up Manetho's idea in spite of the defaming leprosy, as it suited him for apologetical purposes to show the Greeks, who looked down on

118

the Hebrews as a parvenu nation, that the Hebrew people was of a much older pedigree than the Greeks. And now comes in a third party, which usually neither trusts Manetho nor Josephus, and accepts their haphazard theory out of an almost orthodox disbelief in Biblical records!

I do not intend embarking upon a discussion of all the arguments and propositions advanced by the exponents of different theories in connection with the Exodus problem. In order to come to a solution it is necessary to clear away all the heaps of hypotheses under which the real issue is buried and to throw overboard all the ballast of contending views which only lead the student into confusion raising far more his amazement than confidence in view of the considerable amount of erudition and sagacity wasted, to prove things which are not to be found in, or not to be reconciled with, the documents. It is therefore better to abide by the documents themselves, and to draw the picture with the materials they provide. [*See Note* 37, *p.* 223.]

BIBLICAL STATEMENTS AND OUTSIDE EVIDENCE.—For the establishment of an approximate date of the Exodus there are at our disposal the following dates which we give in round figures.

(*a*) A Biblical statement in I Kings 6^1, according to which the temple was built by Solomon in the fourth year of his reign which is about 965 B.C. As it is stated that the date coincided with the 480th year after the departure of Israel from Egypt, hence the Exodus must have taken place about 1445 B.C.

(*b*) The well-known tablets of Tell-el-Amarna in Assyro-Babylonian language and cuneiform writing, discovered 1888 in the archives of Amenophis IV (1375—1350 B.C.). Among them there are letters addressed to him by one of his Palestinian vassals, Abdi-Khiba, ruler of Jerusalem. In them he complains of an invasion by a people called Habiri, who have since been identified with the Hebrews, and asks for an immediate supply of military reinforcements to repel the enemy. The date of those letters can approximately be fixed at about 1370 B.C.

Considering that Jerusalem was conquered for the first time shortly after Joshua's death (Judges 1⁸), the letters of Abdi-Khiba could without difficulty be brought into line with it. The year 1370 would be about seventy-five years after the Exodus, and would very well cover the forty years of the wandering in the desert and the subsequent time between the entry into Canaan and the conquest of Jerusalem. Thus the tablets of Tell-el-Amarna would confirm the date calculated on the basis of I Kings 6¹.

(*c*) The stela of Merneptah (1225—1215 B.C.) son of Rameses II, discovered by Sir Flinders Petrie in his tomb-temple in 1896. It contains a hymn celebrating some of his victories in Libya and other countries. At the end, reference is made to his campaign in Canaan, and the name of Israel is mentioned among the defeated peoples. It reads as follows:

"Canaan is captured with all evil.
Ascalon is carried away.

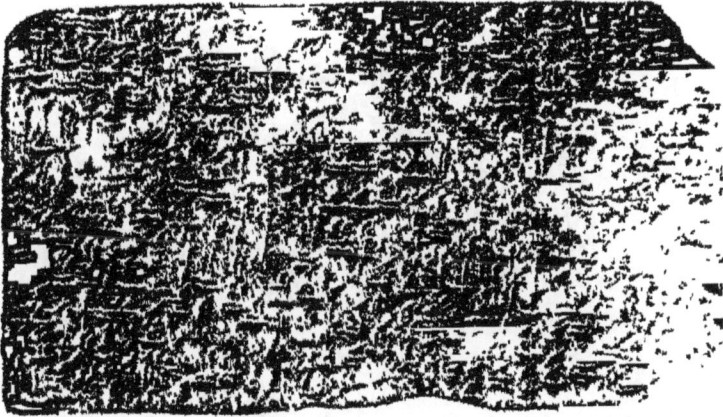

Letter of Abdı-Khıba, Governor of Jeıusalem about 1370 B.C., to Amenophıs IV, Kıng of Egypt, ın cuneıform scrıpt, complaınıng of the ınvasıon by the Habırı (Hebrews) and askıng for reınforcements (see p. 120)

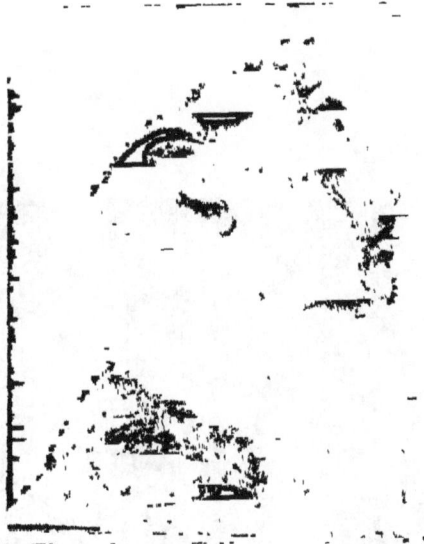

Amenophıs IV, Akhenaton (1375 B C.).

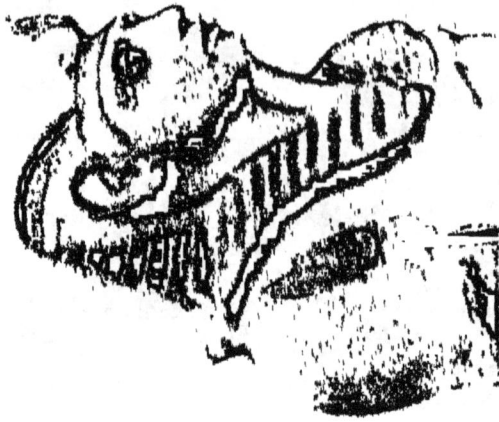

The Pharaoh Merneptah (1225–15 B C), son of Rameses II (see p 120 seq)

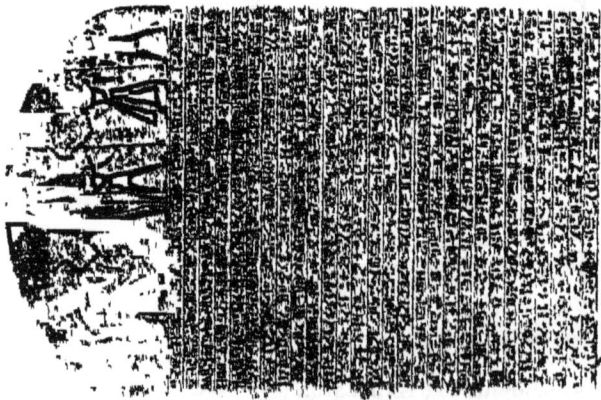

The Israel-Stela in which Merneptah boasted to have annihilated Israel. The name of Israel occurs just in the middle of the second line from below.

Gezer is seized upon.
Yanoam is reduced to nothing.
Israel is desolated; his seed is not."

The inscription is dated from the fifth year of Merneptah, which is approximately 1220 B.C. It is the earliest mention of Israel outside the Bible, and the only Egyptian monument on which it occurs.

Now Merneptah is generally considered to be the Pharaoh of the Exodus, and the reference to Israel in his inscription is connected with the fight between the Egyptians and the Hebrews soon after the Exodus. If this view be accepted, the Exodus must have happened between 1225 and 1220 B.C., which means more than two centuries later than the above-mentioned date, apart from being in contradiction with the route of the Exodus and the time spent in the Desert.

It is around these two archæological documents that a battle has been raging for the last thirty-eight years in connection with the dating of the Exodus. Many endeavours have been made to accord them with the Biblical data but without any satisfactory result. The solution is made still more difficult by the mention of Rameses together with Pithom (Ex. 1[11]) as the store cities built by the Hebrews for Pharaoh. As it happens that no king of the name Rameses is known before the 13th century B.C., and that Rameses II (1292-1225 B.C.) had actually built a town named after him Per-Rameses, i.e. "house of Rameses," scholars, who long before placed the Exodus after Rameses, were induced to identify the store city with Per-Rameses, and to deduce from this circumstance that Rameses was the Pharaoh of the oppression, and his son Merneptah the Pharaoh of the Exodus.

TWO CONTRADICTORY VIEWS.—As it is seen there are two contradictory views that can hardly be reconciled. On the one side is the Biblical dating of 1445 confirmed by the evidence provided by the Tell-el-Amarna tablets; on the other side is the year 1225 B.C. suggested as the date of the Exodus, based on the mention of Raamses in Exod. 1¹¹, and on the Merneptah Stela. Some of those scholars who uphold 1225-1220 B.C. as the date of the Exodus, do not accept the identification of the Habiri with the Hebrews and refuse to connect the Tell-el-Amarna tablets with the conquest of Canaan by the Hebrews. Others do not reject the identity of the Habiri with the Hebrews, but attribute the reference to an invasion at an earlier date. On the other hand, those who are inclined to accept the Biblical date as correct, suggest that there were two Exodus, one about 1445 and a second, complete one, under Merneptah, 1225-1220 B.C. They think that a confirmation of a second Exodus could be found in an inscription of Rameses II recently discovered in *Besan*, the Biblical Beth-shan, in the Western Jordan valley. There it is stated that a great part of the inhabitants were deported by Rameses to Egypt and employed for the construction of large buildings. As the deported are called *Apiri*, they are identified with the Hebrews and it is suggested that they were those who built the Rameses city. It is maintained that the author of the Exodus story, using different sources, could not distinguish between the pre-

The head of the mummy of Rameses
II (1292–1225 B C)

The stela of Rameses II,
found in Bet-She'an, men-
tioning the Apiri (Hebrews?
see p 122 *seq*).

Rameses and the post-Rameses Exodus and thus mixed them together, throwing them both into one Exodus. [*See Note* **38**, *p.* 224.]

DECISIVE EVIDENCE FROM JERICHO.—In these circumstances a decision could only be reached by the discovery of an invulnerable outside proof, either confirming the Biblical statement or favouring the hypothetical views of speculative history-reconstruction. Fortunately such proof has quite recently come forth from the excavations of Jericho. Here it was discovered that the fall of the walls of Jericho as told in Joshua 6²⁰ was not, as hitherto supposed, a grotesque legend of exuberant inventiveness, but a real fact due to an earthquake which destroyed the walls, thus opening the city to the besieging Israelites. The only legendary feature in the story is the belief of the Israelites that the massive and unassailable walls fell to the sound of the trumpets blown by the priests in their processions round the walls.

As Prof. Garstang has shown by unmistakable proof based on pottery and dated scarabs, the earthquake cannot have taken place at any other time than between 1413, the first year of the reign of Amenophis III, and 1300 B.C. Now if we follow the Biblical chronology and take 1445 as the year of the Exodus, and we add the forty years of the wandering in the wilderness, the fall of Jericho must have taken place at about 1405 B.C., and this is exactly within the period assigned by Prof. Garstang to the earthquake at Jericho. This fact can be taken as decisive. It is by itself the strongest evidence of the exactness of the Jericho story we could have ever

123

expected; then it also confirms the Biblical date of Joshua's entry into Canaan, thus throwing a search-light on the whole Exodus problem and the early stages of the conquest of Canaan.

Now if we adhere to any of the views hitherto advanced concerning the Exodus date, we enter a labyrinth from which we cannot get out, in spite of shifting dates, altering Biblical texts and disfiguring statements—methods which became very current in settling diffi-culties in Biblical history. But in accepting the Biblical dates, supported by the finds at Jericho, almost all the difficulties are removed and the way is opened to a satisfactory solution. Accordingly the Exodus has actually taken place as stated in I Kings 6¹, 480 years before 965 B.C., the year of the building of the temple by Solomon, that is 1445 B.C., under Amenophis II. The fall of Jericho, the first city taken by the Israelites, occurred at about forty years later in 1405; and the Tell-el-Amarna tablets, of about 1370 B.C., in men-tioning the presence of the Hebrews in the district of Jerusalem perfectly accord with the Biblical report showing the Hebrews pushing their campaigns from Jericho towards the North and West, and confirm the notice (Judges 1⁸) about the invasion of the region around Jerusalem.

THE ISRAEL-STELA OF MERNEPTAH.—As to the stela of Merneptah, it refers to his fight against Israel a long time after the Exodus. The very fact that Merneptah boasts to have "annihilated the seed of Israel" is a clear indication that the Israelites have already long before been settled in the land having attained a strong hold in the country. This is felt by many scholars, but it is either explained away by denying any importance to the mention of Israel in the Stela, or by contending that here Israel only refers to a part of the Hebrew people, or that the whole Exodus story is only a faded reminiscence of the fight mentioned by Merneptah! But now after the Jericho evidence, the Merneptah campaign cannot be connected with the Exodus but with much later events.

There is, however, another circumstance of great importance: for of the whole area of Palestine and North Syria, from Ascalon in the South, to Yenoam in the Land of Retenu, somewhere near the Lebanon, only Canaan and Israel are mentioned by Merneptah. This can be taken as an indication that the part occupied at that time by Israel must have been of some considerable extent. It is to be remembered that it was shortly after the campaign of Merneptah that the war of liberation set in under Deborah. The raids of Rameses II and his son Merneptah must have struck the indigenous peoples more than the Hebrews, and weakened the oppressors of Israel to such an extent that the courage of the Hebrews to fight for their liberty was more stimulated than ever before. Thus, striding from one victory to another, they achieved their full independence under David and Solomon.

THE CITY OF RAMESES.—The only remaining obstacle to be removed is the mention of *Raamses* together with Pithom as a store city (Ex. 1¹¹), and *Rameses* in connection with Joseph (Gen. 47¹¹), and the Exodus (Ex. 12³⁷), as "the land of Rameses." I personally can see no strong ground why "the land of Rameses" or the City of Raamses must necessarily be associated with the name of Rameses II, only because it happened that we do not know another previous king of the same name. There are about seventy kings who reigned 400 years before Rameses II, between 1900 and 1600 B.C., many of whom are not known to us by name and those who are known bore very genuine Egyptian names like Amenemhet, Senuseret, Apophis and the like. Who will venture to say with absolute certainty that there was not among them also a king of the name of Rameses? And after all, must the city and the land of Rameses be connected by all means with the name of a king? Besides this, I am not at all sure that Rameses, as it is spelt and pronounced in Hebrew, is forcibly identical with the name of the king, as in Egyptian it sounds *ramesse* as well as *ramessu*, meaning: "Ra-has-given-birth" or "Ra-has-been-born." It is thus very possible that there were two different names, so that we would actually have in the "land of Rameses" and in the store city of Raamses a different form from that of the king's name, and consequently could have existed long before Rameses II.

But even if it be admitted that Rameses II and his city of Per-Rameses are meant, they can very well have been introduced later into one of the manuscripts of the Joseph and Exodus narratives by a copyist, or a reader, who lived hundreds of years after they were written. They either replace an old name of the district and the store city, because they were better known at a later time; or they are only marginal additions by a copyist, or a reader, and were then incorporated into the text of the next copy, because they were thought to belong to the original text.

To make it clear by way of analogy: Suppose we found in an ancient Somerset chronicle, which bears all the intrinsic and linguistic marks of being a composition of the 2nd century, the mention that when the Romans settled there they engaged or forced the Britons to build for them the town of *Aet Bathum*, a name for *Bath* which only became customary in the 7th or 8th century in substitution of the old Roman name *Aquæ Sulis*. In such a case no true historian would maintain that the whole chronicle cannot be taken as a composition of the 2nd century, because of the mention of *Aet Bathum*; but he would suggest that it is either a substitute for the older name of the city, or a note originally written on the margin by a copyist or reader of the 7th or 8th century, in order to determine the place by a name which was better known in his time, and then incorporated by subsequent copyists into the text itself. Thus all that could be inferred from the mention of Raamses is that the manuscript, to which all our copies of the Pentateuch go back, originates from the time posterior to Rameses II, but not that the whole story of Joseph and the Exodus *must* have been written after Rameses II, and still less that the *event* of the Exodus cannot have taken place before his time. [*See Note* 39, *p.* 224.]

CONCLUSIONS.—Now the position is clear: on the one

hand we have a clearly defined statement in I Kings 6[1], supported by other evidence, independent of one another, such as the tablets of Tell-el-Amarna and the Jericho finds. On the other hand, there is the mention of Raamses which, if taken as evidence, would fit none of the suggested theories and dates and would lead nowhere. Under these circumstances the statement of I Kings 6[1] has definitely more claim to be considered as a fundamental starting point than the mention of Raamses which, as we said, can easily be explained as accidental, either as a substitute for an old name, or as an additional gloss to the original text, so that its anachronistic character would not in the least upset the structure.

Not only are the Exodus and the subsequent events brought into line with the Biblical statements, but the duration of Israel's sojourn in Egypt, as given in Ex. 12[40], can also be retrospectively established in full accord with the considerations we made in connection with the date of Joseph's advent to office. In adding 430 years to 1445 B.C., the date of the Exodus, we go back to the 19th century B.C., to the time of the great kings before the invasion of the Hyksos about 1780 B.C. on the one hand, and come closer to the time when the Patriarchs settled in Canaan, on the other hand. Thus, from all the theories suggested, the Biblical data prove to be the best founded and to provide the simplest solution of the whole question.

THIRD SECTION

THE EARLY STORIES OF GENESIS

CHAPTER I

ORIGIN AND AFFINITIES

In the foregoing section on the Joseph and Exodus narratives I have shown their close relation to Egyptian language and thought. That this part of the Pentateuch, describing the sojourn of Israel in Egypt, has a certain Egyptian colouring, has been admitted even by those Egyptologists who persistently deny the historicity of the Joseph story and the Exodus.

By the abundant evidence adduced it was shown that the Egyptian influence is much deeper and wider than a mere colouring; in fact, the composition of such accounts becomes conceivable only at a time when the Hebrews lived in Egypt in closest contact with the Egyptians.

Now I propose to show that the Egyptian influence is also apparent in the early stories of the first Book of Moses, although the stories themselves have no connection whatsoever with an Egyptian environment.

The establishment of Egyptian elements in the Creation story, the story of Paradise, of the Flood, and many others, is particularly interesting and important because the modern school of Biblical criticism, with very few exceptions, is still entirely dominated by the Assyriological orientation, which derives everything in Genesis from Assyrian and Babylonian sources.

131

It is true, as we have already observed, that Assyriology has thrown a great deal of light on some parts of the Bible, especially on the story of the Flood. But the very fact that Assyro-Babylonian and early Sumerian myths offer very remarkable parallels to the Biblical Flood story, led Assyriologists and Old Testament scholars to generalise the Assyro-Babylonian influence on the Genesis stories, and to extend it beyond all justifiable proportions. [*See pp.* xxiii *and* 190.]

They were certainly right in assuming that those striking parallels were an indication that the Biblical Flood story especially must have originated in a period when the Hebrews were in immediate contact with Babylonia. But they went wide of the right path. As is well known, there are two periods in which the Hebrews were closely connected with Babylonia. The first was in the time of the patriarchs, when they emigrated from Babylonia between the 20th and the 18th centuries B.C., and the second some twelve to thirteen centuries later, in the Babylonian exile, which began in 588 B.C.

Now instead of tracing the Assyro-Babylonian influence on the early stories of Genesis from the time when the patriarchs left Babylonia (20th-18th century B.C.), Assyriologists and Biblical scholars have adhered to the view that, as a whole, only the time of the Babylonian exile (6th century B.C.) could be considered for the composition of those stories. The only exception is made with that portion of the Flood story which is attributed to the so-called Jehovist of the 9th or 8th century B.C. Thus only the 9th century B.C. is admitted as the earliest

132

possible date for the acquaintance of the Hebrews with a certain part only of the Assyro-Babylonian myths. The idea that this could have happened in the Babylonian period of the patriarchs is rejected as altogether inadmissible, and the whole of the Patriarch narrative is regarded as unhistorical and even as legendary.

THE QUESTION OF ANTIQUITY.—Yet on closer examination of all the Biblical connections with Assyro-Babylonian, I arrived at the conclusion that the Genesis stories cannot belong to that later period, but only to the time of the great civilisation of Ur of the Chaldees, when the first patriarch of Israel emigrated to Canaan. It is there that Mr. Leonard Woolley has discovered traces of a great flood, and it is there that that story, together with some others, must have reached the patriarchs before they left Babylonia.

Moreover, a minute analysis of both the Hebrew and Assyro-Babylonian texts, carried through in *The Lang. of the Pent.* (pp. 103-121) led me to these conclusions:

1. That the linguistic influence of Assyro-Babylonian is much less than has been hitherto alleged, and that even in those portions in which the Assyro-Babylonian influence is most clearly evident, like the Flood story and the story of the Tower of Babel, there are far fewer Assyro-Babylonian elements than might be expected.

2. That even in these latter stories the differences, not only in language, but also in subject matter, are much more abundant than the parallels and resemblances; and finally:

3. That all the differing elements are so thoroughly

alien to Assyro-Babylonian in form and spirit that they must have originated from an altogether different source.

THE COMBINED ASSYRO-BABYLONIAN AND EGYPTIAN CHARACTER OF THE STORIES.—In the course of my studies I have been able to discover many Egyptian elements in the Genesis stories, and found that almost all features which were alien to Assyro-Babylonian were of Egyptian origin. On the one hand, there are striking resemblances and parallels between the Biblical stories and the Assyro-Babylonian myths, pointing to an Assyro-Babylonian influence. On the other hand, the existence of so many Egyptian elements must be taken as an indication of a very intensive Egyptian influence.

Thus we are led to the assumption that actually these stories were originally drawn from Assyro-Babylonian sources, but that they were later overpainted with Egyptian colours and filled with Egyptian elements. The whole picture attained a more Egyptian character in appearance and substance, retaining only the original Babylonian framework, and a few reminiscences from the parent sources.

This is the case also with other narratives of Genesis which have been forced by Assyriologists into an Assyro-Babylonian framework, but actually have lost the last vestiges of connection with Assyro-Babylonian—or, indeed, have never had such relation. There are some, however, which still retain Assyro-Babylonian reminiscences both in language and content, to which Egyptian elements were added when they were fixed in writing in a common Hebrew-Egyptian environment in the Exodus period. A very striking example of such a combination of Assyro-Babylonian and Egyptian elements in a story of early Babylonian origin is offered, as we shall later see, in the narrative of the Flood, and also in that of the Tower of Babel.

In the following section I shall endeavour to show definitely and conclusively the Egyptian origin and character of those elements which are alien to Assyro-Babylonian and that there is a number of typical Egyptian details even in the Flood and Tower of Babel stories which are themselves of Babylonian origin.

CHAPTER II

The Story of Creation

In dealing with some features of the Creation in the light of the Egyptian ideas of creation, I do not propose to discuss the Assyro-Babylonian hypothesis still upheld by Assyriologists and radical Biblical scholars, in spite of my conclusions laid down in my book, *The Language of the Pentateuch*.

One need only compare the Biblical story and the illustrations here drawn from Egyptian sources with the Assyro-Babylonian parallels quoted by Assyriologists, to realise how wide are the divergencies. Indeed, it soon becomes apparent how little illuminating are the Assyro-Babylonian myths for the understanding of the Biblical creation, and that it is the Egyptian background which throws full light on the most important and conspicuous points of creation, and explains many features which have always puzzled the interpreters and theologians. In some instances it gives us the key to the solution of problems which were considered insoluble. [*See Note* 40, *p.* 225.]

THE MONOTHEISTIC CHARACTER ·OF THE STORY.—All this does not mean, however, that the Genesis stories are so substantially dependent on Egyptian as to make them appear as simple borrowings, taken over lock, stock and barrel, from Egypt. By penetrating more deeply into the Egyptian conceptions of creation, and by comparing them with those of the Biblical creation, we realise that the author, though influenced by the Egyptian world of ideas, and imbued with Egyptian views on many details does not follow them in their mythological conceptions. Nor does he accept all the elements which formed the Egyptian universe.

Everywhere he is guided by his monotheistic idea. He eliminates all the mythical features alien to the monotheistic spirit, modifies those elements which could be transferred from the mythical into the religious or ethical domain, and in some cases introduces in the creation such new conceptions as to mark a distinct opposition to Egyptian views.

This independence is also apparent in the art of composition. The author has his own characteristics, a style peculiar to himself, and a language which, though intensively compact and concise, is rich, elastic and realistic.

A SUPERLATIVE MASTERPIECE OF COMPOSITION.—The whole work is a superlative masterpiece of composition, the like of which one would seek for in vain either in Egyptian or in Assyro-Babylonian literature.

One conspicuous result from the study of the Biblical creation in the light of Egyptian is that the monotheistic author built up his world upon a peculiarly new system. While the whole idea of creation among the peoples of antiquity—not only the Babylonians and Egyptians—is based on a narrow local conception, accepting their own "land" as representing the "whole earth" the monotheistic author of Genesis does not limit his horizon to the confines of his land, that is to say, the Land of Promise, which was holy to him. The "earth" meant for him not merely his own "land," but the wide world generally.

Moreover, the whole underlying idea of creation held by other peoples was essentially mythological, each part of the cosmos embodying a divinity. The author of Genesis consciously and deliberately detaches the universe from polytheistic conceptions. Earth and heaven, sun and moon, the stars and the waters are simple component elements of the universe, without any individual will or power, all of them being subjected to the will of the one God and His disposition only.

Another feature distinguishing the Biblical creation from the Egyptian and the Assyro-Babylonian creations, is the purity of mind prevailing throughout the whole story. There is not one trace in the Biblical story of that sensualism by which especially the Egyptian creation myths are dominated; a sensualism nourished by the most repugnant lascivity and stimulated by raging passion. On the other hand, the naturalistic outlook of the Biblical author unfetters the story from the childish and primitive mind in which the mythical creation stories are swathed. [See Note 41, p. 225.]

A NEW COSMOLOGICAL SYSTEM.—One can even say that the Biblical creation is, among all other creation stories of antiquity, the only one which has some approach to a scientific cosmological conception. This is most prominently apparent in the creation of light. Whereas according to the Egyptians it was the sun which first emerged from the chaotic waters to spread light over the earth, in the Biblical view it was a mass of light which first came into being and in which all the heavenly bodies, sun, moon, and all the stars were incorporated. It was only on the fourth day that the "lights of the firmament" were created, and this for the exclusive purpose of dividing the time, in days and nights, months and years. But apart from the logical sequence in causing the lights to be separated from the original mass of light, there is a deliberate opposition to the mythological conception that the sun was the first and most powerful god to appear on earth. As a whole we see herein the first endeavour to establish a cosmological system which is not based on mythological ideas, but which follows an evolutionary view based on a religious foundation.

THE FIRST VERSE OF GENESIS.—We begin with the first verse of Genesis, which reads in the English Bible: "In the beginning God created the heaven and the earth." Simple though this phrase may appear, it has always been a crux to all interpreters of the Bible, because it is contradicted by the second verse: "And the earth was without form, and void." After it is said that heaven and earth were created, how can it continue speaking of a chaotic state of the universe which was previous to the creation of heaven and earth? It is still more astonishing that it was not heaven and earth, but the light that was created before anything was in existence (ver. 3). It was only on the second day that the heaven and on the

139

third that the earth were created. (ver. 7-10).

On close examination of the first word of Genesis in the light of Egyptian texts which refer to the creation of first things, we find that the Hebrew word *berēshīth* "in the beginning," which is derived from *rōsh* "head," is an exact adaptation to the Egyptian expression *tepiyet*, likewise formed from *tep* "head" and extended to the meaning "primeval time, before anything existed." It becomes at once clear that the Hebrew word is not to be taken in the sense of beginning but in that of "earliest time, days of yore, in indefinable primeval time." It is used here exactly as its Egyptian prototype, *tepiyet*, which is particularly typical for Egyptian creation texts.

Thus the first verse of Genesis does not refer to heaven and earth as individual creations, but indicates generally that the creation of the universe took place in primeval time. The translation should therefore read: "In primeval time God created heaven and earth."

The real purpose of the first verse is to serve as a heading for the whole Creation story. The story itself begins with the second verse, and proceeds to describe things in the order they were created.

By establishing the true meaning of the first verse of Genesis, one of the most heated controversies, which for centuries confounded theologians and troubled the minds of believers, is definitely disposed of.

THE TWO SKIES OF THE EGYPTIAN WORLD.—The word for heaven in Hebrew is *shamāyim*. This word is common to all other Semitic languages, but only in Hebrew is it used in a dual and not a singular form, thus conveying the meaning of "two skies." This fact has caused grammarians and lexicographers much embarrassment, to such an extent that different theories are advanced to explain that in this special case this form is not to be taken as a dual.

The matter is, however, very simple. As the Egyptians conceive the cosmos, there were two skies, one covering the earth and the other one expanded over the nether world. When the Hebrews came under Egyptian influence they dropped the word in its singular form as was current in all Semitic languages, and adapted it to the Egyptian conception, using it in a dual form with reference to the two skies. It remained in use among the Hebrews during their long sojourn in Egypt, and became so deeply rooted in their language that, when the author of Genesis wrote the Creation story, he could not give up the word *shamāyim* altogether. But as, on the other hand, he could not admit the existence of a nether world, he had to apply *shamāyim*, in spite of its dual form, to the heaven covering the earth only.

Another interesting example of similar nature is given in the well-known name Elohim for God. Though in a plural form, it is used in a singular meaning, referring to the one only God. Here also we have a use peculiar to Hebrew, and absent in all other Semitic languages.

ELOHIM AS NAME OF GOD.—It is only in Egyptian that the plural *netru* meaning "the gods" was commonly and generally used as a collective term. As a rule, the Egyptian never spoke of God in the singular and, when he referred to a definite divinity, he mentioned it by name, viz., Ptah, Ra, Thoth, Amon, etc. In a general way he used the plural because he had all the gods in mind, or a "corporation" (*khet*) of gods, composing a number of "great gods" (nine or twenty-seven). It is only in later times, not earlier than the twelfth century B.C., that we encounter in Egyptian literature the use of *neter* as a singular for "god" generally, and even this as a rule only in popular literature, not in sacred scriptures.

Now the use of Elohim in Hebrew can only be explained as an adaptation to the early Egyptian plural *neteru* made during the sojourn of Israel in Egypt under the intensive influence of Egyptian conceptions and Egyptian speech. This plural became then so common that the monotheistic author of the Pentateuch had to retain it and apply to the one God, emphasising, as he repeatedly did, that under Elohim the one God solely and exclusively was to be understood, and this is best evidenced by the fact that all the verbs referring to Elohim are in the singular. It is only in this light that the phrase "Jehovah he is Elohim," repeatedly recurring in the Pentateuch, becomes comprehensible.

It was directed against those who still conceived Elohim in its Egyptian sense as a plurality of gods, and was intended to stress the point that, though plural in form, it was singular in meaning, and that the one God was no other than Jehovah.

As is well known, it is generally accepted by Biblical critics that those portions of the Pentateuch in which the use of Elohim occurs are of much later date than

142

those with the use of Jehovah as name for God.

In assuming, as we do, that the use of Elohim as a plural originated in Egypt in a much earlier time than the composition of the Pentateuch, it would *ipso facto* result that the Biblical critical theory about the dates of the Elohistic and Jehovistic authors of the Pentateuch has to be definitely dismissed. Another explanation is to be sought for the alternative use of Elohim and Jehovah in the Pentateuch.

This is not the place to discuss such a very complicated question, but I want to state at once that in the Creation story there can be no doubt whatsoever that the first chapter of Genesis, in which only Elohim is used as the name of God, is an earlier composition than the second chapter, in which the name Jehovah is added to Elohim.

As we shall presently see, there are other reasons which make it certain that the second chapter of Genesis was written after the first chapter, as a completion, and even as a correction, of the first. The importance of these facts cannot be overemphasised, because they give the key to all the problems concerning the composition of the Pentateuch and the religious history of the Bible in general.

CHAPTER III

THE CREATION OF MAN AND ANIMALS

THE TWO VERSIONS OF CREATION.—The remarkable discrepancies between the first and the second chapters of Genesis, especially with reference to the creation of man and animals, has caused insurmountable difficulties to Biblical commentators and to the theologians of both the Jewish and the Christian faiths. We mention here only a few of the most conspicuous cases.

According to the first chapter, verse 27, man was created "in the image of God," and in a very vague and obscure manner, without any particulars, it is said that men were created as "male and female". As to the creation of beasts, the fish and fowl were created from the water and all others from the ground.

Another peculiar feature of the first chapter is that the beasts were created before the man. In the second chapter, verse 7, we are told that man was the first living being, that God formed him of the "dust of the ground," and that he "breathed into his nostrils the breath of life so that he became a living soul."

Here there is no mention of man being "in the image of God" or of man having been created as "male and female." On the contrary, we are told that the man remained for some time single, and that only later was the woman made from one of his ribs. As to the animals,

144

The Ram god Khnum fashioning
the child's body with its double (ka)
on a potter's wheel [See Note 42, p.
225]

they were made after and not before the man (2^{19}).
Further, it is said that "all the beasts of the field and the
fowl of the air" were formed out of the ground and
it was only after they were brought to Adam that they
became "living souls" for which the English version
has "creatures." It will be noted that here the mention
of fishes is omitted altogether.

These two versions of the creation of man and beasts,
showing a different order and disagreeing in the details
of the creation itself, are given together with no
explanation.

MAN IN THE IMAGE OF GOD.—We must ask ourselves
on what theory is each of the versions based, and what
is the underlying *motif* of some of the strange details
given?—for instance the connecting of the name Adam
with Adamāh, which means "red earth"; then the idea

145

that the beasts came to life after having been given a name by Adam, and that the female mate has been created from a part of Adam's body.

Now, if we turn to Egypt, we find a plain explanation of all these questions. First, the idea of the man created in the "image of God" is a typically Egyptian conception. It is often expressed with reference to the gods created by the first primeval god "out of his body." The idea was that as these gods were carnal children of their creator they bore his likeness. This is the conception which underlies the version in the first chapter of Genesis, where the first man takes the place of the first gods as an emanation from God Himself bearing his own image. The difference is that he is not a carnal derivation of the body of God.

His supremacy over all other living beings consists only in his having been created by God Himself in His own image, whereas the others were caused to emerge from the water and the earth. This supremacy conceded to him is further enhanced by the fact that he was the last to be created, as the crown of all creation and the perfection of all living beings, so as to "have dominion over all the earth" (1^{26}).

It is also in line with this conception that man was created as male and female at the same time, being equal emanations from God the Creator. The idea laid down in the first chapter could be characterised as the naturalistic view of creation.

MAN FASHIONED LIKE A FIGURE OF CLAY.—Now there was another Egyptian belief exclusively applied to the

146

creation of man. The god Khnum is the creator of man; he forms the body from clay on the potter's wheel, and after completing the form and countenance the soul is blown into the nostrils. This procedure is performed by him symbolically each time before a child is born, thus giving the newcomer life.

The author of Genesis, in adopting this idea in the second chapter for the creation of the first man, did it with the view of eliminating the conception of equality of body and soul; he ranges the man, in so far as his body is concerned, along with all other creatures, but concedes to him the supremacy with regard to the soul. By doing so he wanted to avert a great difficulty implied in the theory of the first chapter.

The man being a direct emanation from God, it was thought that, like animals, he came into life as body and soul without any interval between the formation of the body and its animation with life. Now it was quite comprehensible and in accordance with observation that the animals, as products of water and earth, should die away body and soul together, in the same way that they came together into being. But how was it to be explained that man also, in spite of being a direct emanation from God, endowed with life as a divine incarnation, could share the fate of animals and die, body and soul?

The dilemma was unavoidable. Either there was no difference between man and the beasts in both body and soul, and in that case man's privilege of being created by God Himself did not offer him any advantage, or man was a divine incarnation and, as he was body and soul a part of God, he ought to be eternal like God.

THE SOUL OF MAN AND THE SOUL OF ANIMALS.—Another difficulty confronted the conception that underlies the account of the creation of man in the first version of Genesis, and it was this: If the carnal part of man was as divine as the soul, either the man as spirit of God's spirit and substance of God's substance could not be tempted by sin, or God ought to be subject to the same temptation—as, in fact, were all the gods of the polytheistic pantheon: nay, they were even more passionate and more sensual than their creations.

But if only virtue and no vice is attributable to God, then some compromise had to be sought to establish on one hand the superiority of man over beasts, and, on the other hand, his inferiority to God. Compromise is made in such manner that the supremacy of man prevails without, however, the danger of his being deified. As body he is part of the earth and perishable, but his soul is divine, a true emanation of the spirit of God. That accepted, the other difficulty also disappears, as the man's disposition to sin is simply given in the earthly origin of his body, whereas the soul is pure and virtuous.

Now we come back to the beasts. Of what origin is the soul of all living things other than man? In the first version they were body and soul of earthly origin, as they emerged as living creatures from the ground or the water.

After accepting the view of the man having been first made of dust as a lifeless figure and afterwards endowed with a soul by a special action of God, and not automatically as it was conceived in the first chapter, the author of Genesis felt the necessity of assuming a similar process with regard to the beasts. This is done in the second version. Here the animals do not emerge from the ground by themselves right away as living beings, but they are first formed from the dust of the ground as lifeless figures, just as the body of the man.

But whereas man was endowed with a soul coming from God and breathed into him by God Himself, the beasts were not animated by the same procedure; here Adam was instrumental in endowing them with life. They were brought to him as lifeless figures, and it was only after he applied to each of them the word "living soul" that life was brought unto them. (Gen. 2^{19}).

This involves that the power which brought them into life was not divine, but an emanation of Adam, as a superior earthly creature endowed with a divine soul. Herein is the difference between the soul of man and the soul of animals. They are inferior to him because they got their life through him.

The passage (Gen. 2^{19}) consequently must read: "And Jehovah-Elohim formed out of the ground every beast of the field and every fowl of the air and brought unto Adam to see what he would call it, and whatsoever (animal) Adam would call 'living soul' that should be its name," i.e. that by virtue of being called so it should become a living creature. The words "that should be its name" do not relate to choosing individual denominations for the animals such as lion, horse, ox, eagle, etc., but imply that by the mere fact of an animal being called a "living soul" its animation should directly follow upon the receipt of this designation. Any animal figure to which Adam would say, "Be thou called living

149

soul," should *ipso facto* become a living being.

This is the solution of the enigma of the two divergent versions in Genesis. In this light, the second chapter, far from being an altogether differing production of another author than that of the first chapter, proves to be a correction and amendment of the first chapter, added by the same author. Thus they are not two contradictory versions by different authors patched together at a considerable later date, as Biblical critics maintain.

ADAM AND THE "RED EARTH."—One of the most remarkable associations of Egyptian ideas with the Creation story is the designation of the first man as *Adam*, and the connection of this name with the Hebrew word *Adamāh* (Gen. 2⁷) which literally means "The red one."

This expression does not exist in any other Semitic language than Hebrew, a fact which suggests that it is a Hebrew coinage. Then the question arises on what conception it was originally based, and what was the underlying idea of the association of Adam with the "red earth."

If we turn again to Egypt, we find that the word *tesheret*, "the red one," designating "sterile, barren land," is in juxtaposition to *kemet*, "the black one," used for "fertile land," as in Egypt only the black muddy soil, inundated by the Nile, is cultivable. Indeed, from the oldest to the latest period of Egyptian literature *kemet*, "the black one," was the common name for Egypt as the fertile land, whereas the antithetical *tesheret*, "the red one," was an expression for "desert" or "foreign

150

countries" inhabited by nomads and barbarians.

In *Adamāh* we have a close adaptation to *tesheret*, and
the connection of Adam with *Adamāh*, "the red one,"
becomes perfectly comprehensible. The first man was
made from the "red earth," the barren land, the soil
not yet cultivable, as stated in Gen. 2⁵. That the
author of this story actually conceived *Adamāh* as desert
land is obvious from Gen. 3²³, where *Adamāh* is used
for the desolate country in contrast to the Garden of
Eden, just in the same manner as *tesheret*," barren land,
desert," was used as a contrast to cultivable land.

It should be noted that Gen. 3¹⁹ expressly says of
Adam that he was made from *Adamāh*, "red earth,"
and (2²³) that he was expelled from "the garden" to
till that "red earth."

When the first conception of the man as being a direct
emanation from God had to be restricted, it was intended
to let him be, in the second chapter, produced from
ordinary unhallowed soil, so as to obviate any possibility of the first man being identified, in a polytheistic
sense, with the Creator. The whole idea was to lead up
to the Fall of Man, and this is clearly conveyed in the
fact that his formation from the "red earth" is particularly
stressed in connection with his expulsion from paradise.

In later phases of religious development in Israel, when
the primitive association with Egyptian conceptions was
no more known, and the danger of man being deified
became remote, the idea of man in the image of God
reappears again, but divested of its original meaning.
It is given a new interpretation as a divine mercy
bestowed upon man, who, in spite of being weak and

151

frail, was brought nearer to God than all the other creatures because of his ability to perceive God's all-wisdom in His wonderful creation, so superbly expressed in the words of Psalm 8[5]: "For thou hast made him only a little less than God (Elohim) and hast crowned him with glory and honour."

THE BREATHING OF THE SOUL INTO THE NOSTRILS.— In Gen. 2[7] the process of animating the body of Adam is described by the words: "And the Lord . . . breathed into his nostrils the breath of life; and man became a living soul." This passage is in every detail in expression and substance typically Egyptian.

To begin with, the expression "breath of life" is the same as the Egyptian *tau en ankh*. Then the idea of

Month, the god of war, holding the emblem of life before the nostrils of the King.

giving a "breath of life into the nostrils" is very common in Egyptian. The whole phrase, both in Egyptian and Hebrew, is literally and grammatically identical. The expression *dy tau en ankh em fened-wy*, "to give breath into the nostrils," is especially frequent in Egyptian literature with reference to gods or kings, emphasising that it is they who give life to man.

So it is said of the god Ptah that he it is who "gives the breath of life into every nose"; or of King Sesostris III that he is "the shepherd who knows how to blow in the breath of life"; or of King Merneptah, "breath enters the nostrils at the sight of him"; or of another king, that "he it is who gives breath into the nostrils of women."

In some cases, the Egyptian has *nifu en ankh*, "air, wind of life," just as *ruah hayyīm* in Hebrew, "wind, air of life" is equal to "breath of life." Thus it is said of Osiris that he "poured forth the air that is in his throat into the nostrils of man."

The cases in which kings or gods are implored "to give the breath of life" or "air of life into the nose" or "into the nostrils of man" are innumerable.

Thus for instance it is said of the god Ptah that he it is "who gives the breath of life to every nose"; or of the King Merneptah that at the sight of him "breath enters into the nostrils"; or of the god Ammon that "he bloweth breath into every nose." On every possible occasion the gods and kings are implored "to give air or breath into the nostrils," especially by war prisoners who beg for their lives. In some cases even the dual "the two nostrils" *fened-wy* is used, just as in Hebrew *appāyyim* "both nostrils".

The idea is also pictorially represented, showing in some cases a god or a goddess holding the emblem of life before the nose of a new-born child, to endow it with life, or of the deceased, so that he "becomes alive again." In other cases it is the king who receives the breath of life into his nostrils from the one or the other god.

As can be seen, the Hebrew-Egyptian relation is confirmed not only by the identity of both the idea and the expression, but also by the fact that it is only the Egyptian that offers such an exact parallel with the Hebrew.

Amon-Ra, king of the gods breathes life into the nostrils of King Thutmosis IV.

THE CREATION OF THE WOMAN.— One would look in vain in all known Creation stories, whether of the Babylonians or of any other of Israel's neighbours, for the background of the idea of a living being having been created from a part of the body of another.

This is, however, furnished in one of the oldest Egyptian myths which deals with the creation of the first gods by Ptah-Atum.

There it is said that the eight great gods who, together with Ptah-Atum, formed the "corporation" of nine gods, were created by him from his members, namely, the god of wisdom and writing, Thoth, from his heart; the god king, Horus, from his tongue; and other gods from his teeth, hands, nose, and other parts of the body.

154

The idea that the first gods, who were considered as ancestors of mankind, originated from parts of the body of the parent god, is typical in Egyptian theogeny. It is clear that only in an environment where such conceptions were rife could the author, in writing the Creation story, have hit upon the idea of bringing the mother of mankind into existence from the body of the first man.

The Egyptian myth also provides us with an answer to the question often asked: Why was the rib chosen for the formation of the woman? This was not, as is often assumed, because the extraction of a rib would not vitally affect the structure of the human organism, but for quite another reason, namely, that the woman should not originate from any member from which the Egyptian gods had been created, so as to eliminate every connection with Egyptian theogeny, and to exclude any association of the mother of mankind with any attribute ascribed to their own or the other deity. To the Hebrew author the creation of the woman from the man's body was merely a symbolical act, and was interpreted by him in a high moral sense (Gen. 2²⁴), namely, as the foundation of union between man and woman.

THE LIVING SOUL.—The expression "living soul" which is peculiar to the Creation story of Genesis, coincides literally with Egyptian *ba ankh*, "living soul." Moreover, the whole phrase, "to become a living soul" (*kheper em ba ankh*) is typically Egyptian and occurs literally in Gen. 2⁷, "and man became a living soul."

It is often said in Egyptian funeral texts that the

deceased goes out as a "living soul" or the wish is expressed that he may become a "living soul." In many pictures one can see the mummy being visited by the soul, which the Egyptians imagined in the form of a human-headed hawk, in order to become alive and go out in the light of the day.

But whereas in Egyptian it has quite a specific meaning, and plays an important role in the destinies of the dead in the nether world, in the Biblical story "to become a living soul" is used only with reference to the earthly life, without any association with after life. It comprises only the time from the moment when the body is endowed with the breath of life until the moment when it is left by the soul. It is remarkable that in Egyptian it is never applied to beasts as is the case in Gen. $1^{20},^{21},^{24}$; 2^{19}.

It will be noted that the English version has in the last-mentioned passages the expression "creatures" or

The soul of the deceased in the form of a human-headed hawk, holding the emblem of life in its claws, hovers over the mummy to awaken it to life

"living creatures" instead of "living soul," as the Hebrew text has it. This substitution of "living soul" by "creatures" or "living creatures" with reference to the animals, is due to the difficulty that was felt in the application in the Hebrew text of the same expression "living soul" to animals and to man (Gen. 2⁷). It was therefore thought that some differentiation had to be made in the translation. But now, after having established the real difference between the soul of man and that of the animals in origin and process of animation, that difficulty is disposed of, and the Hebrew expression "living soul" proves to be right, and can be applied both to men and animals, as it simply means a living being.

BIRDS AND FISHES.—A very striking feature in the first chapter of Genesis (1²⁰) already noted by the earliest commentators is that the birds, like the fishes, were produced from the water and not, as stated in Gen. 2¹⁹, formed from the earth together with the other animals. They are mentioned here with the fishes, and are not even reckoned as earth animals.

This conception is typically Egyptian; for the birds which engaged the interest of the Egyptian sportsman nested in the swamps and bushes of the banks of the Nile, and in the neighbourhood of other waters, these being the only places in the overheated, sun-bathed Nile valley which provide shade and protection.

From the swamps and reeds he first saw the birds fly up. It was between the papyrus rushes and the tall, tangled and twisted plants that he discovered the first

157

nest, and it was there that he saw the baby birds creeping out of their eggs. These observations made him conceive the idea that there lay the cradle whence the birds came into being. The marsh birds were for him the first winged creatures, and he saw the origin of all birds in the swamps and slime of marshlands, streams and waters.

THE WATER CREATURES.—As a matter of fact, in the oldest religious writings of the Egyptians the goose, or the wild duck which is so typical of the Nile swamps, appears quite distinctly as the first living being. We are told that the sun-god Ra who was the first god to make his appearance, crept as a goose from the egg which lay on the mud hill in the midst of the primeval chaotic water Nun.

The idea of a common origin of birds and fishes as water creatures now becomes quite intelligible. This line of thought is best reflected in the fact that in the Egyptian literature birds and fishes are always mentioned together.

It is from this angle that Gen. 1[20] is to be viewed: the first winged beings go forth together with the water creatures, and the former fly above the earth "on the face of heaven."

It adds to the Egyptian colouring that the expression "on the face of heaven" (Gen. 1[20]), as the Hebrew text has it, is a typical Egyptian phrase (her "face" pet "heaven"), and that the Hebrew designation of winged creatures (or the fowl of the air), as "birds of heaven" (Gen. 1[26],[28],[30]; 2[19], etc.) is also quite common in Egyptian (apedu "birds," en-ta-pet "of heaven").

158

Fish and bird hunting (see p 157 seq).

It is noteworthy that the two Egyptian theories above mentioned are reflected also in the terms used for creating in the two versions of Genesis. In the first chapter the typical term employed is *asah*, literally "to do," coinciding with Egyptian *iry*, the word equally used for "to do," and "to create," whereas in the second chapter the word used for creating man and animals is *yazar*, generally applied to the potter's work, thus closely following the Egyptian conception of the second theory of the human body being formed at the potter's wheel.

Another very typical Egyptian feature which appears in connection with the creation of the water animals, is the mention of the *tannīnīm*, Gen. 1[21] (plural of *tannīn*). As the true meaning of *tannīn* is "crocodile," the *tannīnīm* are neither whales, as it is generally rendered, nor fabulous monster creatures, as it is interpreted by Assyriologists and many modern commentators. Also here it refers to the gigantic reptiles of the Egyptian waters, which were considered as the terror of the Nile and the most dangerous water animals. The *tannīnīm* are, thus, real creatures and all the mythological combinations construed around it can be disposed of (see p. 109).

CHAPTER IV

THE STORY OF PARADISE

THE SEARCH FOR THE SITE OF PARADISE.—As we have seen, the contrast between the Garden of Eden as an ideal spot of fertility, and Adamāh, the "red earth," as arid, untilled land, so clearly expressed in Genesis 3²³, is very typical of Egypt, where the fertile earth, irrigated by the river, is muddy and black, appearing like an oasis surrounded by an endless desert.

This being so, the question arises whether the author of Genesis, in writing the Paradise story, did not have in mind the conditions found in Egypt.

A close and detailed study of the description of Eden and the garden planted therein leads to conclusions which justify such an assumption. Many elements in the narrative reveal an Egyptian background, and that in turn reveals the place where paradise was imagined and makes it also possible to solve the problem of the origin of the four paradise streams.

The mention of the Euphrates and the Tigris among the four paradise streams (Gen. 2¹⁴) has led—or rather misled—scholars of all ages to locate the paradise in Mesopotamia. This view was very enthusiastically taken up by the pan-Babylonian school of Assyriologists as a conclusive proof of the Babylonian origin of the whole of the Paradise story. Modern Biblical critics run with

The Egyptian conception of life and work in Paradise, in a garden studded with trees and watered by a river and several canals

them neck and neck along the whole track of Assyro-Babylonian mythology in search of paradise, from the extreme northern boundaries of the two-stream land, where the sources of the Tigris sprang, right down to the Persian Gulf, where the Babylonian paradise, *dilnum*, was supposed to have flourished.

With indefatigable zeal and inexhaustible imagination they discovered and promptly established the Babylonian origin of every detail and every feature of the Paradise story, even in cases which are thoroughly alien to the Babylonian spirit.

EGYPT THE HOME OF PARADISE.—In reality, apart from the two rivers, Euphrates and Tigris, most details of the story point to Egypt as the site of paradise. The first clue is given in the statement (Gen. 2^5) that the earth was not watered by rain, but in a mist, coming up from the ground, and that Eden was watered by "a river" (Gen. 2^{10})—that is one river only, as we shall presently see. These are conditions which apply in much greater measure to Egypt than to Mesopotamia, as the latter had a quite abundant rainfall, so that its irrigation was not exclusively dependent upon its rivers.

In Egyptian poetry it is emphasised again and again that Egypt alone has the privilege of enjoying all divine blessings, because, unlike all foreign countries, it does not depend on rain, but is watered by the very river that comes from the abode of the gods, continuously bestowing upon it all the blessings of heaven and earth. It is Egypt alone that was not left to the mercy of atmospherical changes.

161

These conditions were most eloquently described in a later passage, Deut. 11$^{10-12}$, though in opposite spirit to the Egyptian boast, "For the land, whither thou goest in to possess it, is not as the land of Egypt, from whence ye came out, where thou sowedst thy seed, and wateredst it with thy foot, as a garden of herbs: but the land, whither ye go to possess it, is a land of hills and valleys, and drinketh water of the rain of heaven: a land which the Lord thy God careth for."

It is obvious that this contrast between Egypt and other lands was in the mind of the author in putting the Garden of Eden, exuberantly fertilised by river water, against the dry and barren "red earth" itself, longing for rain. His mind was obviously dominated by the idea that, during the sojourn of Adam in Eden, there was no need for rain because the "red earth" was not inhabited by any human creature.

THE GARDEN PLANTED IN AN OASIS.—A further indication of the Egyptian background of the Paradise story is furnished by the word *Eden* for the region in which the garden was planted. One of the most extraordinary aberrations of Assyriologists in their modes of interpretation is the arbitrary identification of Eden with the Assyro-Babylonian *edū* "desert." In their eagerness to find Babylonian elements everywhere they have forgotten that, according to their own interpretation of Gen. 2^6, the earth was watered, not by mist as it is generally accepted, but by a flood, and that therefore precisely the spot where the garden was planted could not have been a desert.

But as no other word could be found in Assyro-Babylonian dictionaries to match Eden, they did not mind converting a place represented by themselves as being inundated by a flood into a desert. In truth, the word Eden, far from being a desert, means an *oasis*.

The use of Eden in this meaning was general throughout Biblical times, as can be seen from one of the latest scriptures, Ezekiel 36[35], where the prophet vividly contrasts the infinite enjoyments of an oasis and all its delights with the unutterable desolation produced by the dreary sight of a lonely, endless, sun-baked waste.

Other passages in Ezekiel bear evidence to the fact that for the prophet it was Egypt, the classical land of oases, that was thought to be the home of Eden. The connection of the "Garden of God" with Egypt must have been present also to the mind of the author of Genesis, Chapter 13; for, in describing the exuberant vegetation of Sodom and Gomorrah, before they were destroyed (verse 10) he could find no better picture of prosperity with which to compare it than the "garden of God" and the "land of Egypt."

It is only when we assume that he knew the Garden of Eden was in Egypt that he could co-ordinate them both in the simile as the ideal living image of unseen and unheard-of fertility.

THE QUESTION OF THE FOUR RIVERS.—The question, "Where lay paradise?" is as old as Biblical history; but, in all attempts to find a solution, the greatest difficulty has always been the mention on one hand of Tigris and Euphrates, which presupposes a Mesopotamian region for paradise, and on the other hand of Pishon and Gihon, rivers flowing through other lands. The difficulty was still further increased by the assumption that all the four rivers together flowed through paradise itself.

This made it impossible to fix upon a geographical site for paradise, because in no case could the confluence of all four rivers in one place be explained. Mesopotamia could not be taken as the home of paradise, because the other two streams flowed through countries far remote from Mesopotamia, viz., Kush Nubia and Havilah, which lay somewhere else, but at any rate neither in Mesopotamia nor in Nubia proper. Equally it was impossible to take Egypt or Nubia as the site of paradise, because the two streams of Mesopotamia would not fit in.

The solution of the problem in the attempt to identify Pishon and Gihon with Mesopotamian rivers failed to convince even Assyriologists of a more conservative trend, and thus the question as to the identity of those rivers still remains open.

I propose to go straight to the point and examine the Biblical text itself to see whether it really offers a ground for the assumption that all the four rivers flowed through paradise.

It must first be emphasised that in Gen. 2[10] there is no mention of *four rivers* flowing through Paradise. Quite on the contrary, it is expressly stated that "a river went out of Eden to water the garden," which can only mean one river. It is most astonishing that this fact has escaped almost all Biblical students, yet hence the confusion about the geography of Paradise.

164

The four rivers mentioned immediately afterwards actually have nothing to do with paradise itself. The whole passage (Gen. 2$^{10-14}$) does not refer to paradise, but to the relation of the four rivers to that one river of paradise. All that this passage meant to convey was that the one river of paradise gave origin to the four greatest world streams, thus representing paradise as the source of prosperity and fertility for the whole earth.

This interpretation is best illustrated by the conception which the Egyptians held of the origin of the Nile and the connection of its sources with the Egyptian paradise in the netherworld. According to these "the fields of the blessed" which is the Egyptian paradise, were encircled by "a river" (*itru*) that went forth from heaven. In a mysterious way that river reached the surface of the earth, through two spring-holes below the first cataract between Elephantine and Philae and emerged as the Nile.

This idea is pictorially represented in a relief in a small island near Philae, at the first cataract. Under a lofty mass of rocks, the god of the Nile, Haapi, protected by a serpent, is pouring water out of two vases in his hands, symbolising the two sources of the Nile. Thus the Nile was merely the earthly prolongation of the heavenly "river" (*itru*) and the two spring-holes beneath the cataract only marked the place where it came out to the surface.

Herein are the two prominent features dominating the whole hydrography of the Biblical paradise.

The Nile god Haapi, surrounded by
a protective serpent, pours the Nile
upon the surface of the earth out of
two vases, symbolising the sources
of the two Niles hidden in two
caves beneath the rocks

THE LOCATION OF EDEN ON THE TOP OF THE EARTH.—
From the Egyptians' idea of the situation of the nether-
world and their paradise, we can draw the line which
leads to the location of the Biblical paradise.

They imagined the earth in the shape of a longish
trough extending between two mountains, the one on
the eastern and the other on the western horizon.
linking with their extremities the two ends of heaven.

The nether world was in the west, beyond the western
mountain, outside the horizon.

The idea that men at the end of their lives go down

166

like the sun at the end of its course provided the starting point for the belief that there, at the end of the earth, where the sun sets and the glowing heat of the day gives way to an agreeable coolness and refreshing breezes, begins the "western one" (*imentet*) that is the realm of the dead.

There the blessed enjoy all the delights of the Elysian fields. There they seem to be like gods, and like gods they live from eternity to eternity, feeding on the same meats and being drunk with wine and love, luxuriating in all bliss.

For the monotheistic author of the Biblical paradise story there was no realm of the dead, and there could not be a nether world. Consequently he had to reject the idea of paradise being beyond the horizon, outside the earth. He therefore retained only the western direction of the Egyptian nether world with its paradise, but placed the Eden oasis at the western end inside the earth.

The whole picture becomes now clear. In his imagination the Eden oasis lay right at the top of the western mountain, where heaven and earth meet, having behind it the western horizon and in front of it the whole untilled "red earth."

It was in that oasis that the creation of the first man and of all other creatures took place, and there flourished "the garden," as an abode for the first human dweller. The oasis was the first and only fertile place on the "red earth" before rain came and before there was a "man to till the earth."

Everything else was unfertile land, a great wilderness,

167

and that land extended from the boundary of the oasis towards the east, right to the other end of the world.

The idea that the nether-world began on the western horizon was supported by the conception that the nether world, like the earth, was, as we have already observed, arched over by a second heaven. It was therefore logical to fix the beginning of the nether-world at the point where the two heavens met. It is only through this combination that the solution can be found for the question, how it is that the way to the nether world and paradise went through heaven. The western horizon was simply regarded as the line of transition from earth to heaven, and thence to the nether world and the paradise. It is only through the original association of paradise with the nether world that it became possible to imagine that paradise was connected with heaven.

THE FOUR RIVERS DEPARTING FROM THE RIVER OF PARADISE.—As already stated, the text of the Paradise story does not say a single word which suggests that the four rivers were within the paradise; it expressly states that *one* river only ran through paradise "to water the garden." The Hebrew text of Gen. 2¹⁰ does not mean that the division of the one river into four was effected *within* the area of paradise. What it means to convey is that those rivers came forth from that one river after it had left the garden.

The author, following the idea the Egyptians had of the river of "the fields of the blessed," so visualised the continuation of the Eden river, that on reaching the sandy soil of the "red land" outside the oasis it gradually vanished, being swallowed up by the earth on the surface, but pursuing its flow underground. Under the earth, far away from the spot where the river left Eden, it branched off in various directions, until it reached the spots whence it emerged, to flow on the surface of the earth in the different countries.

The fields of the blessed, surrounded and intersected by waters drawn from the heavenly river. The scenes represent the life and occupations of the deceased in the Egyptian paradise.

This conception of a river vanishing in the desert and nevertheless continuing to flow subterraneously is not at all unknown to those acquainted with the contrast between oasis and desert land. A similar phenomenon is especially frequent in calcareous areas, in various parts of the world, where large rivers are sucked into subterranean cleavages and suddenly disappear from the surface, only to reappear a considerable distance away.

169

These new outflows were always regarded as distinct rivers, and even nowadays are so considered by the local population even in some European countries. In this connection, it should be observed that the belief in a subterranean course of the Nile for long stretches was also shared by Greek authors. Furthermore, the idea that distant rivers were connected underground with the Nile, was entertained by them in respect of the Indus, which they considered to be an upper reach of the Nile. The same was believed even much later by Arabic geographers concerning the Niger.

Even as late as the Middle Ages, the general opinion was that the Nile, on gushing down from the Mountains of the Moon ·below the Equator, penetrated beneath the ground only to reappear on the surface after a considerable distance.

It is plain that the author of the Paradise story set out with the idea that the single paradise river was the first stream of the world, and that the greatest rivers of the earth took their birth from it.

UNIVERSAL VIEW OF THE WORLD PANORAMA.—Now we have the one "river" (*nahār*) which went out of the Eden oasis and flowed through the "garden" just as the Egyptian *itru* came out of the nether world and flowed through the "fields of the blessed." Then we have the conception of the Nile taking its origin from that "river" (*itru*) even as in Genesis the four world streams come out from the Eden river.

But, in contrast to the Egyptian, the paradise river did not rise in the nether world—because it did not

170

exist for the Hebrew author—but in Eden, the oasis on the top of the earth. Similarly, he conceived the subterranean continuance of its course, on the one hand, to the spot near Elephantine where it re-emerged as a river of Egypt, and on the other hand further to those points, where the other great world streams burst out from their respective sources to the surface of the earth.

There is another consideration which is worth mentioning and that is the more universal view of the world panorama taken up by the Biblical author. In contrast with the conception of the Egyptians, the Babylonians and other peoples, who regarded only their rivers as heavenly, without giving any thought to the origin of other rivers, the Hebrew writer, while not giving preference to any particular land or river, entertained the idea that all the great rivers of the world known in his time originated in the one paradise river. This is made obvious by omitting to include the Jordan, the main river of the Promised Land, among the rivers connected with paradise, as was actually done much later, in the third century B.C. by Ben Sirach (24^{26}) out of regard for the Holy Land.

THE DIVINE CHARACTER OF THE NILE.—It even seems that the Biblical author was governed by the intention of denying the divine character given by Babylonians to their rivers, and in a much higher degree by the Egyptians to the Nile, because the Nile was the great god Happi, the "creator of all good things," and so indispensable that "if he had been overthrown in

171

heaven, the gods would fall upon their faces and all men perish."

It is a very striking feature of the whole Paradise story that there is nothing which would indicate reverence for paradise as a sacred place. All the author is concerned to show is that paradise should have served as a place in which men should live a pure life, sharply contrasting with the life of the gods and the blessed in the Egyptian paradise, an attempt which, however, failed because of the Fall of Man.

THE RIVERS PISHON AND GIHON.—As to the rivers of Pishon and Gihon, mentioned among the four rivers of paradise (Gen. 2$^{11-13}$), they were from of old placed in different parts of the world.

Thus, for instance, in the first Greek translation of the Bible (about 200 B.C.) and in the Wisdom of Ben Sirach (24^{27}) Gihon was identified with the Nile, and the Pishon, in the time of Josephus (Ant. I. 1, 3) with the Ganges.

Later they were placed in Armenia, in Persia, and even in Mesopotamia, although the latter was already represented by the Tigris and the Euphrates.

Most fantastic views were taken by some pan-Babylonists, who dominated the field for many years and are still holding the ground. They even transferred the area of paradise to the cosmos, seeking in the main paradise stream the Milky Way, and visualising some other things in paradise which make the strangest cabalistic and allegorical interpretations appear far more reasonable and acceptable.

This is not the place to discuss the matter in detail. The fact that the Tigris and Euphrates, two of the four rivers, were then the greatest streams known in one part of the world, suggests that the remaining two, Pishon and Gihon, must equally refer to other great world rivers in some other parts of the earth. On this assumption the choice of the Nile as one of them was perfectly right. Nevertheless, opinions differed as to whether the Nile was the Pishon or the Gihon.

THE NUBIAN NILE AND THE EGYPTIAN NILE.—Now if we turn again to the text of the Bible, without losing ourselves in speculation, we find that the Gihon is described as flowing round Kush, which can only mean Nubia or the Biblical Ethiopia. It is thus obvious that Gihon can only refer to the Nubian portion of the Nile and it remains to localise the course of the second river, Pishon, which is described as flowing through a country where there was good gold, bdellium (resin) and precious stones (Gen. 2^{12}).

Bearing in mind that the richest and most famous mines of fine gold and the other products mentioned were in the district between Assuan and Coptos (known to-day as Kuft), we are justified in assuming that in Pishon we have that portion of the Nile which extends from Assuan northwards, flowing towards the Mediterranean.

The difficulty of dividing the Nile into two streams is at once removed when we become aware that the Egyptians actually considered these two portions of the river as two different streams. Thus the Hebrew writer

173

was in perfect conformity with the idea which the Egyptians had of the Nile from the time they became acquainted with the countries beyond Assuan, throughout the New Kingdom, the period of Israel's sojourn in Egypt. The description given of the course of each of them exactly tallies. [*See Note* 43, *p.* 225.]

Pishon, the Egyptian portion of the Nile, is that which "compasseth the whole land of Havilah, where there is gold," that is, from Assuan northwards through Egypt proper; and Gihon, the Nubian portion of the Nile, is that which "compasseth the whole land of Kush," that is, Nubia, or the Biblical Ethiopia.

These two streams were supposed to be the nearest to the Eden oasis, and are therefore mentioned first. They were the two largest streams on the one end of the world in the extreme west, and formed the counter-pair to Tigris and Euphrates, the two largest streams of the other end, in the extreme east.

THE MEANING OF PISHON AND GIHON.—By the identification of Pishon it becomes possible to detect the origin of this name. Taken as a Hebrew word it means literally the "increasing, the swelling-up one," characterising the overflowing of the river; and this is exactly the meaning of Haapi, the Egyptian name of the Nile, viz., the "overflowing," the "inundating one." Hence Pishon is nothing else but a Hebrew translation of Haapi.

This view is still further strengthened by the fact that when the Egyptians mentioned Haapi, they had in mind just that stretch of the Nile which we identify with Pishon. No other Hebrew word could therefore be a

174

more adequate equivalent of Haapi than Pishon.

The same can also be said of Gihon. Like Pishon, it is a Hebrew name given to the Nubian Nile; but in this case the author of the Paradise story seized upon a feature which differentiated the Nubian from the Egyptian stretch of the Nile.

Whereas the latter was the "increasing, overflowing one," the Nubian Nile presented another particularly striking phenomenon, having mighty cataracts with tumbling waters, leaping billows and rushing rapids. It was just this feature which the Hebrew writer wished to bring out in coining the name of Gihon, which means the "great burster" the "great leaper." [*See Note* 44, *p.* 225.]

CHAPTER V

The Trees of Paradise and the Serpent

THE TREE OF LIFE.—The "fields of the blessed," the Paradise of the Egyptians, furnish some parallels which can enlighten us concerning the nature of "the tree of life" and "the tree of knowledge of good and evil," in the Garden of Eden.

Just as in the Garden of Eden there was "every tree that is pleasant to the sight and good for food" (Gen. 2⁹), so also the "fields of the blessed" and *ken neter*, "the garden of God," had all kinds of trees with "sweet fruits" (*bener*), such as sycamore, fig, date and vine, as well as lovely (*nedzem*) and "holy" (*shepset*) trees.

Of the first importance, however, is the fact that among the trees of the Egyptian paradise there was also a "tree of life." The idea that the food of the gods provided eternal life was quite natural, and was not confined to Egypt; it was common also to the mythology of the Babylonians. But whereas the Assyro-Babylonian expression "food of life" is quite different from the Hebrew, the Egyptian *khet-en-ankh* "tree of life" literally corresponds to the Hebrew *etz-ha-hayyim* "tree of life."

We find the *khet-en-ankh* mentioned as early as the Pyramid texts, where the wish is expressed that "the king may be fed from the tree of life so as to live from that from which the gods live." A later text says that

176

The tree of life.

"the deceased may be given the food of the gods from the tree of life in order that he may live on the same food."

The Egyptian tree of life had another use. Inscribing the name of the Blessed on the leaves of the tree of life, secured their remaining eternally alive.

The picture here given shows the tree of life. Beneath it Rameses II is sitting on his throne, with the crown of the gods on his head, the king's whip and the emblem of life in his hand. In front of him is the goddess Seshat, "the mistress of writing." Behind her stands Thoth, the scribe of the gods, and on the other side the god Atum, with the double crown of Upper and Lower Egypt. All three are inscribing the name of the king on the leaves of the tree to endow him with eternal life.

177

Nut, emerging from the sycamore, offers bread and water to the soul, imagined in the form of a human-headed hawk

THE TREE OF KNOWLEDGE.—In the same region of the Eastern heaven, where the tree of life stood in the Egyptian paradise, there was also a lusty sycamore. To it was assigned extraordinary importance as being the seat of the gods, as appears from numerous passages of funeral texts, and especially as the seat of the supreme god Ra.

The goddess Hathor is represented as the native goddess of the sycamore. In some pictures of "The Book of the Dead" she appears beneath the sycamore or among its branches; in one of them the deceased is seen at the edge of a pool of water kneeling beneath a sycamore and holding in his right hand a bowl, into which Hathor pours water from a vessel.

In another funeral papyrus it is Nut, the goddess of heaven, who appears as a goddess of the sycamore or the *persea* (a laurel tree). Here, too, the deceased person is seen kneeling beside a pool out of which a sycamore

178

grows. The goddess Nut emerges from the branches and with one hand pours water from a ewer into his hand, and offers him cakes with the other hand.

In one of the tombs we see the deceased beside his mother and wife, sitting beneath a sycamore. Human-headed soul-birds stand before an altar table set with all kinds of food and drink. The goddess Nut offers the deceased water and food; his soul-bird is also refreshing its heart with the same gifts.

There are other fine and most vivid representations of a paradise, with wonderful groves of sycamore, palms, and other fruit trees in the tombs. In one of them, the deceased and his wife are sitting beneath sycamores being fed by a goddess with the fruit of the trees.

The veneration of the sycamore as a sacred tree is very ancient and can be traced as far back as the early Dynasties, 3000 years B.C. Its figs were considered as the most luscious food of the Beyond, and were offered as delicious food to the dead. Moreover, the gods had a special predilection for the sycamore figs; they descended upon the sycamores to enjoy the fruit.

That the deceased should eat this sweet fruit beneath a sycamore, in the midst of the divine beings surrounding it, was the highest bliss of the "glorified and blessed" in the heavenly paradise. Together with it the fig and wine are mentioned as food and drink of gods and dead kings, "the beloved of the gods," who are represented in their paradisial life leaning on their sceptre, clothed in red linen, living on figs, drinking wine like water, and anointing themselves with fine oil.

179

THE TREE OF LOVE.—The most important point for our investigation, however, is that the sycamore always figured in Egyptian love poetry as the love tree, and its fruit as the love fruit. Aspiration to enjoy sycamore fruit and wine in the fields of the blessed is thus closely connected with the yearning for the enjoyment of love, which is expressly mentioned as one of the chief blisses in the Beyond among gods and men. The lover is compared with the fig tree, whereas the "little sycamore" symbolises the beloved bride and speaks out her heart's wishes to her lover. With the tree's whispering that is "as sweet as pure honey," it lures the lover to its cool shadow for the love potion, and he hastens to it, "drunken without having drunk."

From this and other passages in Egyptian love poetry, the sycamore and fig tree appears as poetical and eschatological symbols of love, stimulating passion and filling the hearts of gods and men with joy.

Now it was long ago suggested that the tree of knowledge of good and evil was a love tree, either a fig tree or a vine tree, so the whole episode which led the first men to become conscious of passion and sin was prompted by the love fruit enjoyed by them.

That in the Biblical paradise the fig tree substitutes the sycamore can be explained by the fact that whilst the sycamore was characteristic of Egyptian poetry, in Hebrew poetry the fig was symbolical as a love tree (Song of Songs, 2¹³). This because in Canaan the fig was more frequent and more popular. Therefore it became even proverbial of the fertility and beauty of the land (Deut. 8⁸; I Kings 4²⁵, etc.).

The goddess Nut, from the sycamore,
pours water into the hands of the
deceased, and offers him food. His
wife is seen behind him sipping the
sweet juice of the holy tree.

In the light of all these observations, the mention of
the fig leaves in the Paradise story (Gen. 3⁷) assumes
special significance. It is a clear indication that the
author, in the moment when he lifts the veil of mystery,
hints at the kind of the tree of knowledge by mentioning the leaves.

In connection with this an explanation may be given
of the expression (Gen. 3⁸) "the cool of the day," which
is generally accepted to refer to the cooling down of
the glowing heat of the day. This conception is based
on the interpretation of the Hebrew text, which literally

181

reads "the wind of the day," as meaning the breeze which breaks in towards the end of the day. In reality such a conception does not fit into the conditions of a tropic country. The "wind of the day," or the breeze, is more likely to be expected in the early morning before the start of the heat. It is therefore more adequate to think of the episode as having occurred in the early morning. In a very discreet manner the narrator hints at the early hour, when the human couple awoke with the day and became conscious of what they had done.

The Babylonian sacred tree providing food to the gods and spirits   (See Note 40, p 225.)

THE SERPENT AND THE WOMAN.—From the Egyptian world of the gods we are able to gather a clear idea of the nature and character of the Serpent, and its role with the woman.

Just as, everywhere in Egypt, snakes creep about undisturbed in fields, gardens and oases, and climb freely on walls and trees, so in all pictorial representations of the Egyptian nether world they appear in its gardens and groves, gates and entrances, as well as among its high and stately trees.

182

In almost all of these cases it is not a fantastic monster, but the common uraeus snake, and in rare cases a viper, Even the serpents represented here and there as fabulous creatures are not grotesque dragons, as in Babylonian mythology, but have as a rule the appearance of large boa serpents, sometimes with human legs or wings and the like.

It was such a kind of serpent that the Hebrew author of the Paradise story had in mind.

But whereas the serpent of the Egyptian myth usually appears as a rebel, in eternal conflict with gods and men in the nether world, the paradise serpent is represented rather as a companionable and sociable being, benevolently disposed to man. In the express mention that the "serpent was more subtil than any beast of the field" (Gen. 3¹) its character as an insinuating and fascinating creature is brought out.

It is not the aggressive serpent of the myth, but the magic snake of the fable. It talks to the woman in an attractive familiar way, like all the animals in Egyptian and Biblical fables, and thus secures the confidence of the credulous woman.

THE SERPENT AS LORD OF FOOD.—It is very interesting to note that according to old Hebrew traditions the serpent, before it was cursed, was conceived to be a huge creature walking on legs, just as it appears in Egyptian representations of fabulous serpents in the nether world. It is very tempting to compare the paradise serpent with the one depicted on a sarcophagus with human arms and legs, standing in an upright attitude before a deity and putting a round-shaped cake in its mouth.

The serpent is described as "lord of food." This is very significant, because when we bear in mind that it was the role of the serpent to supply the gods with food in the nether world, it becomes clear why, from among all the "beasts of the field" it was precisely the serpent which was chosen to approach the woman to talk to her about the fruit of the garden without arousing suspicion or alarm in her. [See Note 45, p. 226.]

A Serpent with human arms and legs placing bread in the mouth of a deity.

THE FIGHT BETWEEN SERPENT AND MAN.—There are some other features attributed to the serpents in the nether world which offer parallels to the role of the serpent in the story of the Fall of Man. Thus, as an illustration of the mode of fighting between man and serpent, the man stepping on the snake with his heel and the serpent biting him on his foot, we can adduce a pictorial representation of the serpent in conflict with the sun-god Ra in various funeral and magical texts.

For instance, in the Book of the Dead of Any, or of Khu Nefer, there are scenes showing the combat between the serpent and the sun-god Ra. The serpent, as the personification of night and darkness, rises every morning to fight against Ra at the moment when he is about to go up to the horizon.

Fight between the snake and the cat, personifying the sun-god Ra

It is very characteristic of the Egyptian mind that Ra is here represented as a cat, obviously in association with the idea of its hostility to the snake. In the picture here shown we see the black snake, mad with rage, hurling itself against the cat, as the personification of Ra, just at the moment when it emerges from the holy tree *ished* in order to lift the sun above the horizon. With convulsive coiling body it attempts to bite the cat on the paw. But the cat strikes it with one paw on the head, and with the knife in the other it cuts off its head, the blood spurting forth in great jets.

Many other scenes of the nether world show the dead piercing the head of a snake with a long spear or pointed stick. In all these scenes we have a vivid illustration of the description given in Genesis 3¹⁵ of the fight between man and serpent.

"SON OF THE EARTH."—A very remarkable parallel to the condemnation of the serpent to the eating of dust (Gen. 3¹⁴) is provided in an Egyptian myth where the servants of Ra are entrusted to the care of the earth god Geb, and he is commanded to impress upon them to guard against harming anything whatever. It is said there that their sustenance shall be Geb (i.e., earth dust). Moreover, the serpent is described as being the "son of the earth," because it lives in the earth, and feeds in the earth.

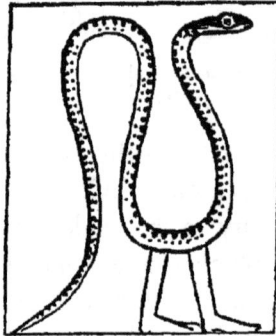

The serpent "Son of the earth" (sā-ta) with human legs

Another very peculiar expression describing the crawling and creeping of the snake as "going upon its belly" (Gen. 3¹⁴) exactly corresponds to the Egyptian expression applied to reptiles as "going upon their bellies." This is the same expression as used for reptiles in Leviticus 11⁴², where it is a distinctive classification of reptiles as a special category of animals.

We draw special attention to the serpent scene, reproduced from an Assyro-Babylonian cylinder in many modern Biblical commentaries and introductions in connection with the Fall of Man. No other pictures than those of the Egyptian and Assyro-Babylonian

A scene of a serpent behind a woman in a garden from an
Assyro-Babylonian cylinder (see p. 186 *seq*)

Thoth, the god of scriptures and scribe of the gods, fixing the
span of life whilst the child is being formed by Khnum on a
potter's wheel (see p 145).

Hieroglyphic text from The Book of the Dead referring to an
Egyptian Flood, first and second lines from left (see p 197 seq)

serpent scene are more appropriate to show how close are the affinities of the Biblical story and Egyptian, and how completely differing is the character of what Assyriologists and Biblical critics think to be an adequate illustration of the episode of Eve with the serpent, some of them considering it even as the very source from which the author of the Fall of Man drew his inspiration. Whilst the Egyptian representation so smoothly fits into the whole atmosphere of the story, supplying most suggestive, even fascinating, details, the Assyriologists themselves are not at all in a position to say what the Assyro-Babylonian scene means to represent, and only quote it because it happens that a serpent is seen behind a lady, apparently carousing with her companion in a garden! Are they a royal couple in a drinking bout, or a god and a goddess before a sacred tree? Indeed, the whole exuberance of pan-Babylonistic imagination was necessary to see in this cylinder any approach to the Genesis story. [*See Note* 40, *p.* 225.]

CHAPTER VI

The Flood Story

AMONG all the Genesis stories, that of the Flood is the only one to which there are some tangible and really substantial Assyro-Babylonian parallels.

The discovery of the Gilgamesh epic, one of the finest pieces of Assyro-Babylonian literature, has brought to our knowledge one of the many flood stories which, from the earliest times, long before Ur belonged to the Chaldees (about 2200 B.C.), was current in Mesopotamia, and of which later several other fragments in various versions have been found.

In that epic, there are passages which so closely. resemble the Biblical account of the Flood, in the course of events and in details as well as in style of narration, that there can be no doubt concerning the original · connection between the two.

THE GILGAMESH EPIC AND THE FLOOD.—The most conspicuous parallel between the Gilgamesh epic and the Bible narrative is found in the passages relating to the sending out of the winged messengers from the ship. The former reads (eleventh tablet, III):

"When the *seventh* day arrived
I sent forth a swallow, letting it free.
The *dove* went hither and thither;

Not finding a resting place, it came back.
I sent forth a swallow, letting it free.
The swallow went hither and thither;
Not finding a resting place, it came back.
I sent forth a *raven*, letting it free.
The raven went and saw the decrease of the waters.
It ate, croaked (?), but did not turn back.
Then I let (all) out to the four regions (and) brought
an offering.
I brought a sacrifice on the mountain top."

The parallel Biblical version is set out in Gen. 8^{7-12},
which reads:

7. "And he sent forth a *raven*, which went forth to and fro,
until the waters were dried up from off the earth.
8. "Also he sent forth a *dove* from him, to see if the
waters were abated from off the face of the ground;
9. "But the dove found no rest for the sole of her foot,
and she returned unto him into the ark, for the
waters were on the face of the whole earth: then
he put forth his hand, and took her, and pulled
her in unto him into the ark.
10. "And he stayed yet other *seven* days; and again he
sent forth the dove out of the ark;
11. "And the dove came in to him in the evening; and,
lo, in her mouth was an olive leaf pluckt off: so
Noah knew that the waters were abated from off
the earth.
12. "And he stayed yet other seven days; and sent
forth the dove; which returned not again unto
him any more."

Further, Gen. 8$^{18-20}$ read:

18. "And Noah went forth, and his sons, and his wife, and his sons' wives with him:
19. "Every beast, every creeping thing, and every fowl, and whatsoever creepeth upon the earth, after their kinds, went forth out of the ark.
20. "And Noah builded an altar unto the Lord; and took of every clean beast, and of every clean fowl, and offered burnt offerings on the altar."

TRACES OF THE FLOOD IN MESOPOTAMIA.—Recent excavations by Mr. L. Woolley in Mesopotamia led to the discovery of traces of a great flood, which must have been so disastrous for the whole country that, to those who survived the catastrophe, it must have appeared to have been universal, sweeping away all that existed upon the face of the earth.

But in spite of so much that points to a common origin, a comparison of the linguistic elements shows that there are only a few expressions in the Biblical story which can be derived from Assyro-Babylonian. Such, for instance, are *tehōm*, "the deep" (Gen. 7^{11}), borrowed from *tamtu*, ocean; *kōfer*, identical with *kupru*, pitch, bitumen; or *gōfer*, the equivalent of *giparru*, a kind of tree or reed from which the ark of Noah was built (Gen. 6^{14}). [*See Note* 46, *p.* 226, *also p.* 133.]

EGYPTIAN ELEMENTS IN THE FLOOD STORY.—This in itself shows how little justified is the opinion of those Assyriologists who represent the Biblical Flood story as

190

completely Babylonian in essence, style and language, to such an extent, that some of them even speak of its being a literal translation. In truth, the few expressions and episodes common to both the Bible and the Babylonian stories can only be considered as remnants from the Babel sources. They by no means justify the misleading course which converts the Biblical story into a Babylonian one.

At the first glance, it is most astonishing that in a narrative originating, as this does, from Babylonia, the most important object in the whole story, the ark (Gen. 6^{14}) is not designated by any of the Assyro-Babylonian words for ship—not even by the word *elippu*, by which the ship of Ut-Napishtim, the Babylonian Noah, invariably is designated, and which also appears as a loan word in later Hebrew in the form of *ilfa*.

It is the Egyptian word *tēbā* which is used, meaning box, chest, coffer, and applied to a ship. Nor is the word *abūbu* the regular expression for the Babylonian flood used in the Bible narrative, but the word *mabbūl* (Gen. 6^{14}, etc.), which means an abundance of water, applicable both to "inundation" and to "overflooding" caused by a sweeping rainstorm.

THE BUILDING OF THE ARK.—Now a close study of the Biblical Flood in the light of Egyptian offers striking evidence in support of our thesis, namely that those parts of Genesis which originated in Babylonia, or had a close connection with Babylonian myths, have later been substantially transformed by the introduction of Egyptian elements grafted on to the Babylonian original.

191

The fact that for the ship an Egyptian word is employed makes it evident that the choice of such a word cannot be accidental, but must be intentional. It can only be explained on the assumption that the author envisaged the whole story as an Egyptian would see it. Consequently he conceived the ark as a large Egyptian barge, a kind of box-ship, consisting chiefly of a large rectangular chest; and he therefore used the Egyptian word *tēbā*, as it was current for "box" among the Egyptians and the Hebrews in Egypt.

The combined Assyro-Babylonian and Egyptian character of the Flood narrative is clearly revealed in the building of the Ark.

Whereas the word employed for the Ark is Egyptian, the words "*gōfer*" for timber and "*kōfer*" for pitch are, as we have seen, the Assyro-Babylonian "*giparru*," meaning reed, wood; and "*kupru*," a kind of bitumen, with which the Babylonian Noah, Ut-Napishtim, is said to have pitched his ship "from within and without." On the other hand not only the shape of the ark but also the manner of making its timbers water-tight are specifically of Egyptian carpentry technique.

This is evidenced by the word *kinnīm* (Gen. 6[14]); it does not mean rooms or cells, but refers to papyrus fibre employed for stopping the joins between the planks, especially of light river boats or skiffs, and also for all kinds of cane work, nets, armchairs, litters and the like, which were therefore called in Egyptian *keniyyu*.

It now becomes clear that the English translation of Gen 6[14], "rooms shalt thou make in the ark," is wrong, and is due to misconception of the word *kinnīm*, as meaning nest, cell, whereas actually it points, as I said, to the Egyptian mode of making the boat water-tight, and not to the divisions within the ark. Then the true translation should be "Fibre-tight shalt thou make the ark."

An Egyptian boat of Thutmosis III, one of the Pharaohs of the Oppression, 15th century B C. The cabin has the door at the left side, and two openings beneath the roof, exactly as in Noah's Ark

EGYPTIAN DESIGN OF THE ARK.—Another feature of Egyptian construction is furnished by the injunction (Gen. 6¹⁴) that the Ark should have a *zōhar*, which is rendered in the English version by window proper, as in the same Flood story 8⁶ not *zōhar*, but the common word *hallōn* is used. *Zōhar* actually denotes a kind of skylight, or dormer, characteristic of the Egyptian houses and temples. It consists of a longish square or semicircular opening, divided by two or three stones or bars, rarely more than half a foot in height. It is situated over the door or in a corner, fairly near the roof, in order to admit the light from above, when windows and doors have to be shut against overbearing heat or driving rain.

This is clearly indicated in Genesis 6[16], where it is said that the *zōhar* should not be more than a cubit in height, and that it should be fixed high up, that is to say, beneath the roof, in order that the ark might be lighted from a spot where no water could penetrate. This provision was necessary, as the window proper (*hallōn*) had to remain closed during the whole time of the Flood. Also the expressed provision for fixing the door at the side of the ark (Gen. 6[16]) is peculiarly characteristic of Egyptian architecture. This may be seen in many pictures of ancient Egyptian houses, particularly those of the New Kingdom, the period of Israel's sojourn in Egypt, where the door is not in the centre but at the end of the house front near the corner.

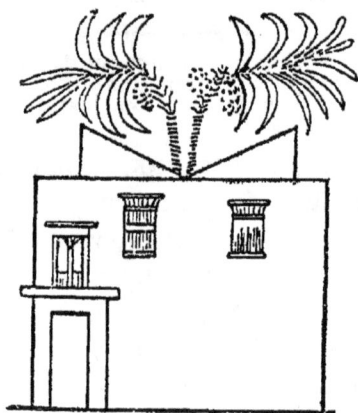

A house of ancient Egypt showing the same architecture as the boat, with the door at the side and openings beneath the roof

THE FLOOD AS RAINSTORM AND AS INUNDATION.—A further striking example of the introduction of Egyptian elements into the original Babylonian framework of the Deluge narrative, is provided by the specific expression *mabbūl* for the Flood. The choice of this word is significant, for it helps us over a great difficulty involved in the Flood story, which contains two different and seemingly contradictory accounts.

One of the strongest bulwarks of Modern criticism against the authenticity and unity of the Pentateuch composition, and for the attribution of the text to different times much later than the Exodus, is the fact that in the Flood story two different versions are distinguishable. The one (Gen. 7⁴ and ¹²) represents the Flood as a torrential rainfall which lasted for forty days.

"4. For yet seven days, and I will cause it to rain upon the earth forty days and forty nights . . ."

"12. And the rain was upon the earth forty days and forty nights."

In the other version, to which Gen. 7¹¹ and ¹⁸⁻²⁰ belong, it is said that the abyss of the great deep burst; and that great floods were forthcoming which inundated the whole earth, thus representing the Deluge as an inundation.

"11. In the six hundredth year of Noah's life, in the second month, the seventeenth day of the month, the same day were all the fountains of the great deep broken up, and the windows of heaven were opened.

"18. And the waters prevailed, and were increased greatly upon the earth; and the ark went upon the face of the waters.

195

"19. And the waters prevailed exceedingly upon the earth; and all the high hills, that were under the whole heaven, were covered.

"20. Fifteen cubits upward did the waters prevail; and the mountains were covered."

In this last version, not only is the first period of the inundation fixed at 150 days (Gen. 7²⁴) thus differing from that of the rainstorm, which is said (7⁴ and ¹²) to have lasted only forty days, but a whole chronology is built up for the Flood, dividing it into different phases, extending over a whole year. Besides these main differences, there are other details in which the two versions differ.

All this provided a pretext for Biblical critics to cut the whole story into pieces, and to detect different authors to whom each portion has to be allotted. The manner in which the Flood story is treated is a good example of the arbitrary handling by the critics, whose methods of dissecting the text result in a confusion which is far more difficult to overcome than that caused by the textual differences themselves.

In truth, the composition of the story cannot be assigned to a later date than the Exodus, nor can it be ascribed to different authors, though originating from two sources.

As has been mentioned, the word for flood is *mabbūl*, and is used correlative to the other word *gēshem*, which means rainstorm. These two terms mark the double nature of the flood as a rainstorm and an inundation caused by flooding from the fountains of the "great deep" (Gen. 7¹¹ and ¹⁸⁻²⁰).

Now, in so far as the Deluge is described as a strong rain which poured forth from the openings or "windows of heaven" (Gen. 7¹¹ and ¹⁸⁻²⁰) the story agrees with all the Sumerian and Assyro-Babylonian versions, by which the Deluge is distinctly characterised as a sweeping rainstorm. But there is no indication in all those versions of an inundation.

Now, while we can find no sure parallel for an inundation, either in the linguistic use or in the content of all the Babylonian flood stories, we are furnished by Egyptian with a solid basis and a clear background for the Flood as inundation; and we are offered, in addition, other points of contact which in many respects are of great importance for the Bible narrative, as we shall presently see.

In a passage preserved in two papyri of the Nineteenth Dynasty (1350—1200 B.C.) the content of which is, however, of much earlier period, reference is made to the discord among the children of the goddess of heaven, Nut, with Osiris. There is an allusion to a great tide, by which the world was completely inundated and brought back to its original chaotic state, when the primal water, Nun, actually filled the whole of the universe.

There the following words are put into the mouth of Atum, the god creator:

"Forsooth, will I blot out all that I have made. This land will perish in the Nun through a flood, as it was in its primal beginning; I alone shall remain with Osiris."

Now for inundation we have in both texts the word *huhu*, which frequently occurs in the meaning of flood, inundation, and has as its basic meaning "to flow, to stream." It is used also for the overflow of the Nile. It has therefore a complete equivalent in the Hebrew word *mabbūl*, covering both the meaning of a "sweeping flood" and of a great "inundation," and has the same basic significance of "streaming and flowing." The choice of *mabbūl* for the Deluge, and not of an expression more in accordance with the Assyro-Babylonian *abūbu*, "rainfall, rainstorm," points strongly to the influence of an Egyptian environment.

This is just the new element which was introduced into the older Hebrew tradition of the Babylonian story. In the particular description of *mabbūl* as an inundation caused by the bursting forth of "the fountains of the great deep" on one side, and as a strong downpouring rain (*gēshem*) coming from "the openings of heaven on the other side", two elements are combined, of which one belongs to the Egyptian and the other to the Babylonian Flood story.

Thus the confines of the waters of both Heaven and Earth broke simultaneously, and the downpour of a

A large Babylonian ship of the time of Sennacherib.
[*See Note* 40, *p.* 225]

198

terrific cloudburst, together with the raging current of a mighty flood, rushed over the earth in order to destroy the whole generation that God had made.

THE WINDOWS OF HEAVEN.—As to the use of the expression "windows of heaven" in the English version, it is to be noted that it is derived from a misconception of the Hebrew word *arubboth*, which is usually interpreted as outlets for smoke, or chimneys. In reality, it is, however, applied in the Bible (Hosea 13³), as well as in post-Biblical Hebrew, for round openings on the roofs, or spyholes, for drawing out the smoke, as they are still to be seen in peasant houses in Palestine and elsewhere. In order to form a correct idea of such spyholes in connection with heaven, one has to think of the domed roofs of interior rooms in large buildings, to which several round openings covered with thick glass or crystal are fitted to let in the light, so, as for instance, in Turkish baths or in huge oriental palaces. Similarly the dome of heaven was conceived as a cupola, stretched over the earth with round holes through which the stars shine. These holes are meant by *arubboth*, and it was through them that the rainstorm of the Flood was believed to have poured down.

CHAPTER VII

The Flood and the Nile

DURATION AND PHASES OF THE FLOOD.—FROM all that has been said it becomes clear that the differences or discrepancies in the Flood story are not to be explained as a patching together of parts by many authors. It is the work of one author, who blends together two stories, the one Babylonian and the other Egyptian into one.

Moreover, it is far from being the case that this story belongs to a period later than the Exodus, because the Egyptian filling-in offers a distinct demarcation from the date of the Babylonian framework.

It can only have been written at a time when the author was very well acquainted with the Egyptian source, and when the Egyptian influence was so intense and so widespread among the Hebrews that the grafting upon it of Egyptian elements could pass unnoticed.

We shall soon see that the fixing of a year for the duration of the Flood and the consecutive phases into which the Flood is divided, are entirely based upon Egyptian conceptions. In fact only one who lived in Egypt, and was acquainted with all the conditions and dates of the rise and fall of the Nile, could have adopted the scheme found in the Bible narrative.

And here we come to discuss the most typical Egyptian element which has been introduced into the original

200

Babylonian story. It is a new revelation which is as marvellous as it is simple. It does away with all the difficulties involved hitherto in the calculation of the Flood year, and leads, as does every discovery of plain and simple facts, to the full truth.

The only clear points of importance in the dates of the Flood are the following:

1. That the duration of the Flood extended over a complete year.

2. That this year begins on the seventeenth day of the second month (Gen. 7¹¹) but does not end on the same day, viz., the seventeenth of the second month in the following year, but on the twenty-seventh (Gen. 8¹⁴), that is ten or eleven days later.

3. That the rise of the water from the beginning of the Flood until it reaches its highest point lasts 150 days (Gen. 7²⁴).

THE "SECOND MONTH" IN THE FLOOD.—Now as in the Pentateuch, and in the Bible throughout, the "first month" always refers to the first spring month, the "second month" here can only mean the second spring month, and not the second winter month.

Accordingly the flood must have begun in spring, and not in winter as one would have expected, considering that the Flood story originated in Babylon, and that there, and in all neighbouring countries, including Palestine, the rain period actually begins in the second winter month and terminates after about five months.

This difficulty has always been felt, but all the attempts to adjust the start of the Flood to the beginning of winter are in open contradiction to Bible reference to the "first month." Moreover, the view that the Flood actually began in the second spring month is also maintained by the tradition in the Book of Jubilees, 6¹⁷.

It is obvious that in accepting the second spring month for the beginning of the flood, neither the climatic conditions of Babylonia nor those of Palestine can have been in the mind of the author of the Flood story. It is incomprehensible that the Flood should have begun in spring and extended over the summer, and not taken place in winter.

THE ANNUAL OVERFLOWING OF THE NILE.—Now a fundamental question in the interpretation of the Flood story is whether there is a definite system by which the duration and the dates of the Flood are reckoned. Or, are the figures given merely haphazard? Is it possible to find an acceptable basis for them? And, if so, what was the system?

If we believe that the conception of the Flood as an inundation has been taken over from Egypt and interwoven in the Biblical narrative, the question arises whether the various phases of the Nile inundation in its rise and fall have not offered the basis for the computation of the Flood year and the consecutive phases of the Flood.

Indeed, turning our eyes to Egypt and the Nile, we arrive at the surprising fact that the chief and most important data of the Flood, as given in the Bible, agree in a most remarkable manner with those of the overflowing and receding of the Nile until again it is at the lowest level.

202

Since the Egyptians believed that the Nile began at the first cataract near Assuan, their interest was naturally concentrated on the time when the Nile began to overflow at that northward point. Consequently we need consider the rise and the fall only on the stretch from Assuan downstream to the Mediterranean.

RISE AND RECEDING OF THE WATERS.—Only the extreme time limits for the onset and recess of the Nile flood are to be considered, not the mean dates, which, until modern times, were utterly unknown. It is obvious that only the earliest date for the beginning and the latest date for the end of the Nile flood would be impressed upon the mind of the average man, and therefore only these would be retained in his memory.

Now it has been established by statistical observation and measurement extending over thirty-six years at various points, as recorded by Sir H. G. Lyons, in his book *Physiography of the River Nile*, that the extreme time limits for the start of the Nile's rise at Assuan lie at the beginning of May (about the fifth) and for the highest flood level at the beginning of October (about first or second). In Lower Egypt, say at Memphis or Heliopolis, in the vicinity of Cairo, these limits are deferred for about eight or ten days, so that the start of the rise is only noticeable about the fifteenth or seventeenth of May, and the highest flood about the twelfth of October.

The flood level remains fairly constant till the beginning of November, and then gradually recedes till the end of December. When in January the river returns to

203

its bed it is once more at its ordinary normal level. It then goes on falling slowly from the second half of January until the middle or fourth week of May, when it reaches its lowest level.

But even after the river has returned to its ordinary bed in January, the soil remains slimy beneath the hardened surface until the seed has taken root in two or three months. It is only then that it gradually dries up completely.

THE FLOOD YEAR AND THE NILE YEAR.—Now, accepting our view that the author of the Flood story took the Nile flood as the basis of his calculation, everything at once becomes clear.

1. The duration of the Flood extends to a full year, like the Nile flood.

2. The 150 days of the rising of the Flood correspond to the period within the two limits between the onset of the rise of the Nile in Lower Egypt at the middle of May, until the highest water level, towards the middle of October, that is exactly five months.

3. The recession of the Flood begins after the expiring of 150 days and is carried out in three stages. First, the water falls by fifteen cubits, so that the highest mountain peaks become visible on the first of the tenth month (Gen. 8⁵); then the water recedes further till on the first of the first month of the following year it dries up from the surface of the earth (8¹³), though the ground still remains moist; finally also the moisture vanishes, and on the twenty-seventh of the second month (8¹⁴) complete dryness ensues.

4. It becomes evident also that the sequence of months remains consonant with the customary usage in the Pentateuch and the Bible generally, that the first month actually marks the beginning of spring, so that the Flood started in the second spring month, just at the time when the rise of the Nile sets in.

5. That the additional ten or eleven days, from the seventeenth to the twenty-seventh, prove that the Flood year is not a lunar year of 356-7 days, but is a full year of 365 days. This is of the greatest importance for solving the calendar problem of the Pentateuch, viz., whether it is to be taken as a lunar or a solar year.

Now it appears clear that only by calculating the chronology of the Flood on the basis of the rise of the Nile, can it be explained why the Deluge took place in summer and not in winter. Even the exact dating of the seventeenth day of the second month could tentatively be explained on the assumption that the Flood was assigned by the author to a year which according to his reckoning began six or seven weeks before the onset of the rise of the Nile in Lower Egypt.

The dates May and October are of course the most important as they coincide with the rise and increase of the Flood. But even for the period of recession of the Flood the Biblical author follows the successive stages of the fall of the Nile, viz.:

1. The soil begins to be visible when the river returns to its bed, for which it requires a period of over two months.

2. The time when the soil is still sodden lasting about three months till the seed takes root.

205

3. The time of about six-eight weeks till the soil is completely dried out by the sun.

THE HIGHEST POINT OF THE FLOOD.—The Biblical author had to find some mark for the highest rise and lowest fall of the flood respectively. He took the highest mountain summits in substitution of the top edge of the Nile bank, where the overflow actually begins, and calculated the recession of the Flood from the level of the mountain peaks to the lowest places of the earth in accordance with the receding of the Nile from the edge to the lowest position.

The substitution of the highest edge of the Nile bank by the highest mountain peaks is astonishingly confirmed by another figure in connection with the Flood, which had never been appropriately explained, or is simply explained away as arbitrary. Nevertheless, it marks an indispensable link in the successive phases of the Flood. This becomes plainly clear through comparing the Flood with the Nile overflow.

According to Gen. 7[20] the water of the Flood rose fifteen cubits above the highest peaks of the mountains. This height coincides very remarkably with the highest level of the rise of the Nile, which from very early times has been established as fifteen cubits, with fractions. Until to-day fifteen cubits and two-thirds is regarded as the requisite measure of a favourable overflow for the adequate irrigation of the Nile area! Conditions in the Nile valley have remained stable through thousands of years.

On the oldest traces of water-gauge marks still

preserved from the age of Sesostris II (1715-1713 B.C.) on the sandy stone rock at Semne, not far from the second cataract, and on the nilometer constructed by the Caliph Suleiman in 715 on the Isle of Roda in Cairo, the highest points marked are fifteen cubits and some fractions.

The step tower of Ezagila (reconstruction by
Professor Unger) "with its top as high as heaven"
It was about 295 ft. high, and was built through-
out with small bricks.

CHAPTER VIII

The Tower of Babel

THE HIGHEST AND MOST FAMOUS TOWER OF BABEL.—In the
Biblical legend the traces of Babylonian origin are still
clearer than in the Flood narrative. That this should be
the case in a short story of only a few verses (Gen. 11$^{1-9}$)
is easily explained by the fact that the scene lay in
Babylon itself.

Hence, the phraseology right at the beginning of the
narrative (Gen. 11^3) coincides almost literally with
building inscriptions of the temple Etemenanki of
Ezagila, the chief temple of Babylon, and those found in

208

other temples, vast buildings and royal palaces in that country.

The material, sand bricks and sun-dried bricks, used for the building of the tower is typically Babylonian, and the expression (Gen. 11⁴) that "its top may reach unto heaven" recalls similar phrases repeatedly employed in describing the height of the very same step-tower of Etemenanki, the top of which was made as high as heaven (*reshīsha shamāmi* exactly as in Hebrew, *rōshō ha-shamāymah*). Even such an expression as "let us make us a name" (Gen. 11⁴) is a typical phrase occurring in many building inscriptions including one of the temple of Ezagila.

The remarkable fact that the whole story of the Tower of Babel is told in the same style and with the use of almost the same words as are found in the Babylonian building inscriptions gives clear evidence of the affinity of Hebrew and Assyro-Babylonian, and even of their identity in mode of speech.

From these parallels it is apparent that we have before us ancient expressions which were current in Babylonia from the earliest epochs. We may, therefore, regard them as reminiscences of the time when the story in its original Babylonian attire came to the notice of the patriarchs when still in Mesopotamia.

It may be added that the Babylonian stamp is revealed quite at the beginning of the story, where it is said that they wanted to build "a town with a tower." This was more typical in Babylonian town building than anywhere else.

THE CANAANITE TYPE OF THE TOWER.—In view of such a close affinity with Babylonian, one would hardly expect that elements alien to Babylonian environment should be contained in this short story. Nevertheless, the central feature, the tower, is not conceived by the author in its characteristic Babylonian form, namely as a step tower (*zikkurat*) as the original legend certainly had it, but as a four-cornered fortress tower, which was common in the Asiatic border lands of Egypt, as well as in Egypt itself. That is plain from the fact that the tower is not called by a Babylonian name, but by *migdal*—a Canaanitish word for "tower" which was widely used in Egypt, especially during the New Kingdom, the period of the sojourn of Israel in Egypt. [*See Note 47, p. 226.*]

There is another and still more palpable influence of the Egyptian surroundings to be found in the story, namely in the explanatory remark (Gen. 11³) that in the building of the tower, bricks (*lebenā*) were used instead of stone, and slime or bitumen (*hemār*) instead of mortar or loam (*hōmer*). Such an explanation can only have been intended for a people among whom the use of bricks for monumental buildings such as a tower was unheard of. It appeared necessary to the author that he should point out that in Babylonia, even for gigantic buildings like this tower, bricks were used, and not stone.

For the same reason he added that in place of the loam which was common in Egypt, in Babylonia bitumen was used for brick building, whereas in Egypt this was only employed where timber joints were made tight, for

210

pitching of ships, for sealing of coffins, and the like.

Bitumen was, indeed, in common use in Babylonian buildings. It is repeatedly mentioned in texts referring to the restoration of the tower of Etemenanki of Ezagila, and in an inscription of Nabopolassar, where it is stated that he caused bitumen (*kupru*) to be used, and pitch (*iddu*) in such great quantities "as a downpour from heaven without measure, and as a devastating flood of water."

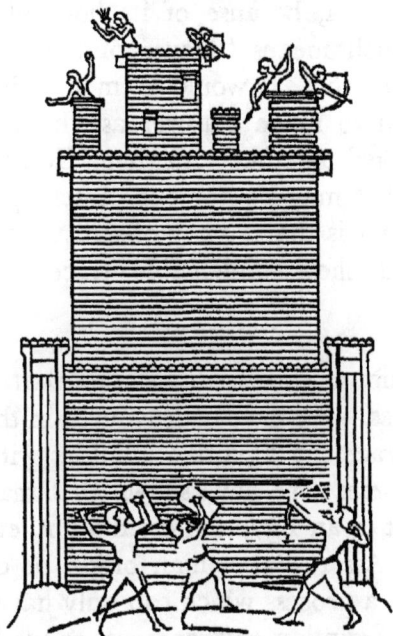

A Canaanite tower (*Migdal*), from a battle relief of the time of Rameses II, 13th century B C

THE ORIGINAL TOWER OF BABEL.—As to the Tower of Babel itself and its origin, most scholars identify it with the above-mentioned step tower of Etemenanki, the

Ezagila temple. This tower was widely known just at the time of the Patriarchs, and the temple itself was familiar long before Hammurabi, the great legislator and real founder of Babylon's power (about 2100 B.C.).

It would be only natural that the legend should have grown round the highest, the most famous and most important tower of those times. It is not unlikely that the original legend was intentionally fashioned round the temple of Ezagila, because of its boastful name Ete-menanki, which means "House of the foundation of heaven and earth." It would seem plausible that the arrogant plan to make a tower as "high as heaven" should be linked together with that "House."

However that may be, for our present purposes, the important point is that a story of a distinct Babylonian origin should show undeniable traces of Egyptian influence.

THE RELIGIOUS AND ETHICAL CHARACTER OF THE GENESIS STORIES.—We have endeavoured in the foregoing chapters to trace the Egyptian affinities with the early stories of Genesis. We have shown that many features in them point to an Egyptian orientation, even in cases in which an Assyro-Babylonian origin or colouring is incontestable, a process which can only have developed in a Hebrew-Egyptian environment, as we have maintained throughout our demonstrations. This logically leads to the conclusion that such a development can only be matured and materialised in the period of Israel's sojourn in Egypt and that it is not hitting far from the mark when we uphold our view that the Genesis stories have received their present literary form close on the time of the Exodus.

Though some mythological reminiscences are still discernible in them, they all bear the original stamp of a new unexcelled creation of the Hebrew monotheistic spirit. The attempts of modern Biblical critics and Assyriologists to see in each detail mythological features, and to convert even plain things into myths, are not based on the Biblical text, but lie in tendencies altogether alien to the book of Genesis and the Bible as a whole. These methods of *mythologising* the Genesis stories are a reversal of the true aim of their author, because they introduce into his work some of those mythological conceptions which he was most anxious to eliminate, and add to them new mythical elements which never had any connection with the Bible. This does not only mean a falsification of the spirit of the Bible, but also the construing of a fanciful Hebrew mythology which nowhere existed but in the whimsical imagination of its exponents. The facts are quite to the contrary: even in cases where there is a mythological background it has been broken up and shattered in its foundation. [*See Note* 48, *p.* 226.]

This tendency of the writer of Genesis is everywhere clear, namely, to denude all the myths used by him of their polytheistic elements and mythological character, so as to render them fit to be embodied into the framework of his monotheistic teaching for the building up of a new religious and moral conception.

The mythological character is transformed into an ethical one. All the primitive and brutal ideas present in

213

the polytheistic myths are converted into pure moral impulses for the promotion of good and the defeat of evil. All the struggles of superior and inferior gods, tormented and torn by jealousy, fear and mistrust of each other, every one of them striving to secure for himself sole dominion in heaven and earth, are here transferred to a higher spiritual sphere, and are presented as the eternal conflict between the evil instincts of sinful man and the divine purpose to free him from vice, and to render him the perfect medium of purest virtue.

It is here that lies the permanent significance of the Genesis stories, and it is their deep religious and moral meaning which always made them, and still makes them, attractive and instructive to the devoted believer and the simple reader, to the literary man and the critical student. It also does not affect either the originality or the intrinsic value of the Genesis compositions whether this or that story originated in the one or the other literature, whether this or that detail can be derived from this or that source, and whether certain features are or are not new forms of otherwise legendary or mythical conceptions. What really matters is that here, as everywhere in the Bible, the underlying idea and the dominating *motif* is to lead the world into the right direction by revealing the sources of evil and destruction, and pointing to the path of good and life, truth and justice.

NOTES

NOTES

Translations of almost all the Egyptian tales and texts quoted, or referred to, are to be found in: A. M. Blackman, *The Literature of the Egyptians* (1929), being a translation of A. Erman, *Die Literatur der Aegypter* (1923), and in J. H. Breasted, *Ancient Records of Egypt*, 5 vols (1906-7) those of Assyro-Babylonian texts in: R. W. Rogers, *Cuneiform Parallels to the Old Testament* (1912).

1. I purposely avoid adopting the pronunciation *Yahweh* or *Yahvistic* which became fashionable among Biblical critics, because it is based, as I shall show in the second vol. of *The Language of the Pentateuch*, on an erroneous interpretation of this Divine name.

2. This attitude is chiefly due to the fact that almost all the leading Egyptologists of the modern school accepted the theories of Biblical critics without having sufficient knowledge of Hebrew and even of the Bible. This could not be better confirmed than by the astonishing, though very polite, hint made by the well-known Orientalist, E. Littmann, in his review of Erman's new edition of his Egyptian Grammar to the fact that the prominent Egyptologist mistook two of the most elementary Hebrew pronouns as being generally *Semitic*, not realising that they are peculiar to Hebrew (*Zeitschrift für Semitistik* 1929, *p.* 224). It is not difficult to imagine what an Anglicist would think of a Germanist who would describe *what* and *that* as *Germanic*, not being aware that in this form they are only used in English.

3. It is obviously due to deductions drawn from the allegations of certain Egyptologists that even such an eminent scholar and cautious critic as S. R. Driver

repeatedly stated in his *Introduction* to the Old Testament and comments on the Joseph and Exodus narratives that the number of Egyptian loan words in the Pentateuch is so negligible, that a direct Egyptian influence on Hebrew can be discounted, or that the allusions made in them to Egyptian life and customs are not of a kind to prove the author's close and personal cognisance of the facts described. Such statements show best the value of conclusions derived from second-hand knowledge.

4. Gen. 11[81] and 12[4] suggest that Aramaic was the language of the Patriarch in Haran; and Gen. 31[47] marks the time when Canaanite was already adopted, as the name given to the heap of stones by Jacob was *galeed*, which is a Canaanite-Hebrew word, whilst the name chosen by Laban was the Aramaic *Yegār-sahadūtha*. Deut. 26[5] the first Patriarch is called an *Aramean*, for which the English Bible has *Syrian*.

5. Many noteworthy contributions from more recent time are to be found in: H. J. Heyes, *Bibel und Aegypten*, 1904; M. Kyle, *Moses and the Monuments*, 1920; J. A. Frank-Knight, *Nile and Jordan*, 1921; A. Mallon, *Les Hébreux en Égypte*, 1921.

6. Among the high dignitaries of Pharaoh's Court there was also a "chief hair-dresser of Pharaoh" (*mer iry sheny per' ō*). Specimens of razors can be seen in all larger museums.

7. It seems that also the antithetic term "years of plenteousness," Gen. 41[34, 53] corresponds to the Egyptian *sa*, "a plenteous (year)," from *say*, "to be satisfied," just as the Hebrew *sōba'* is also derived from *sābā'*, "to be satisfied."

8. The English Bible has: "and they cried before him, bow the knee." This translation is based on the assumption that the word *abrekh* is of Hebrew origin derived

218

from the root *barakh*, "to kneel down." But this view is untenable especially from a grammatical point of view, as *abrekh* can never be an imperative. It was therefore rightly suggested that it must be an Egyptian word, and Spiegelberg's identification with Egyptian *ib-rek*, "heart to thee" (*Egyptologische Randglossen zum Alten Testament*, 1904), is the most plausible.

9. The English Bible has: "Shall all my people be ruled," but as I have shown in *The Lang. of the Pent.*, p. 7, the Hebrew expression *nashak* means literally "to kiss," and is an adoption of the Egyptian word *sen*, "to kiss," which was metaphorically used for feeding.

10. It is noteworthy that the Hebrew word *adōn*, "lord," was also common in titles (*idn*) of the Egyptian administration. This word of Semitic origin was like many other Semitic loan words in use in the New Kingdom in the period of Israel's sojourn in Egypt.

11. Readers of the English Bible will have to bear in mind that the character of Egypt as "two lands" is not apparent in the translation, for the obvious reason that it is only through the Egyptian equivalent that the true meaning of *misrāyim* as a "twinland" is revealed.

12. Also among the priestly titles, there was that of "the feeder of the two lands" (*se-dzefa-tawy*). This title does not only accord in conception with Joseph's description as "feeder of the two lands," but even the component elements of the title are the same as in Zofnat (*dzefa-en-ta*) "the food of the land," only that in the title the first word is the causative form of *dzefa*, and *tawy* is the dual of *ta*. It may be added that in one picture the goddess Sekhmet is seen presenting to the lips of a high dignitary the golden neck chain as a symbol possessing the magical power of nutrition. This is a clear indication of a connection between the func-

tion of the "feeder of the land" and the symbolical significance of the golden neck chain.

13. The Hebrew expression *magōr* means "sojourning" and is applied to the duration of life on this earth. The rendering "pilgrimage" conveys the same meaning, but is not a literal translation.

14. See Sir E. A. W. Budge, *The Mummy*, for a full description of rites and ceremonies, also J. Garstang, *The Burial Customs of Ancient Egypt*, and Sir G. Elliot-Smith, *The Royal Mummies* and *The Egyptian Mummies*.

15. This is the literal translation of the Hebrew text and the allusion is to the father ready to receive the child on his knees. On no account can "the knees" refer to those of the mother.

16. See Wetzstein, *Die Syrische Dreschtafel,* in *Zeitschrift für Erdkunde*, Berlin, 1871, on the various usages made in Syria of the thrashing board.

17. The Hebrew expression could also mean "chief of the cooks," but it is more likely to mean "chief executioner," as II.Kings 25⁸. This corresponds to the Egyptian title *wdza'yu*, slaughterer for executioner.

18. It may be mentioned here that in the tale of the Two Brothers it is said of a princess that she rode on horseback behind Pharaoh. Although the papyrus is a copy of the twelfth century B.C., the tale itself is of the eighteenth and even of the nineteenth century B.C.

19. See about the real meaning and usage of "unto this day," *The Lang. of the Pent.*, pp. 254-8, where it is shown by a great number of parallels from Egyptian texts that this phrase is an adaptation to Egyptian being used in a more general way without limiting it to a definite time.

20. See Sethe-Partsch, *Demotische Bürgschaftsurkunden*, p. 169 sq. In this most important collection there is

much material about the agrarian conditions in Egypt.

21. This is not the only example of his misunderstanding the true spirit of the Biblical narratives. Similar misinterpretations can be found also in his comments on the episodes of Jacob with Esau, Gen. 27 and 32-33.

22. See the translation in R. W. Rogers, *Cuneiform Parallels to the Old Testament*, 1912, p. 135.

23. See about labour conditions in ancient Egypt: Spiegelberg, *Arbeiter und Arbeiterbewegung*, also Erman-Ranke, *Aegypten und Agypt. Leben*, p. 139.

24. See Sir Flinders Petrie, *Israel in Egypt*, and V. Z. Trumper, *The Mirror of Egypt in the Old Testament*. Of special interest are his observations on the connection between the plagues and the Egyptian gods. This conception is clearly expressed in the "great judgments," Ex. 6⁶, 7⁴, directed against the gods as is apparent from 12¹²: "and against all the gods of Egypt I will execute judgment." For the Egyptian colouring of the phrase, see *The Lang. of the Pent.*, p. 80.

25. The equivalent of the Hebrew word *Kussémeth* is *spelt* as it is rendered in the Luther Bible and alluded to in the Authorised Version, and not rie (rye) as in the Revised Version. Rye (*secale cereale*) is a European product which has never been cultivated in Egypt; and, as far as I am aware, is not even now known there, whereas spelt, a kind of cheap wheat (*triticum spelta* L., or *triticum decocum*, which the Egyptians called *bedet*), was thousands of years B.C. the chief nourishment of the greatest part of the land population of the Nile Valley. Grains of spelt have been frequently found in miniature granaries offered to the dead from the earliest times of Egyptian history.

26. The sandals were taken off by the Egyptian when

entering the house and put together with the walking stick on the floor or on a chair, just as it is done in England with the gloves and walking stick.

27. In this connection it may be mentioned that *goblet* for little cup is derived from Hebrew *gobī'a* as the English Jews pronounce *gabī'a*.

28. "The showing" is an elliptic expression. Originally it must have been *maa her*, "showing the face," as it is still preserved in the more complete *ankh maa her*, "mirror showing the face," or "to see the face." The Hebrew follows the elliptic expression.

29. The Egyptians sometime used *irety*, "the two eyes," for sun and moon, as the eyes through which the heaven looked upon the earth. Thus the Hebrew simply passed the metaphor to the earth as the sun being the eye through which the earth looked out.

30. In the inscription of King Neferhotep in Abydos (M. Pieper, *Mitteilungen der Vorderasiatisch-Aegyptischen Gesellschaft*, vol. 23, 1929, p. 4), Horus is described as *gereg-tawy*, "the founder of the two lands." This explains best the connection between the reign of Horus and the "foundation of the two lands" expressed in our passage.

31. See W. Spiegelberg, *Recueil des Travaux . . . Egypt. et Assyr.*, Vol. 25 (1903), p. 184 sq. and Vol. 28, p. 163 sq., chiefly based on an earlier essay, by F. Chabas, *Sur l'usage des Bâtons de main chez les Hébreux et dans l'ancienne Egypte*. A more specified substantiation of the details given here, supplemented by some more features of the rod will be given in the second vol. of *The Lang. of the Pent.*

32. The word *medu* also occurs in the Egyptian proper name *nes-pa-medu*, "he who belongs to the (holy) staff (Spiegelberg, *Nöldecke-Festschrift*, under No. 96). This name is also reproduced in cuneiform script as *ish-pi-*

mattu. The transliteration of the last element confirms the correctness of the Hebrew form *matteh*.

33. The paraphrastic translation: "and I made it (the river) for myself," is a makeshift. The true meaning: "I made myself," the only exact rendering of the Hebrew text, is confirmed by the conceptions the Egyptians had of the divinity of the kings, to whom they attributed all the powers of the gods. In mythological texts it is often said that the primeval god begot himself (*wetet su-dzesef*), that he gave birth to himself, that he created his own form and that he is the fashioner of his own body, ideas which are most clearly reproduced in the phrase the prophet attributed to Pharaoh.

34. It must be pointed out that the forms *tannīn* and *tannīm* are identical as appears from Is. 27¹ and Ps. 74¹³. Here as in many other similar cases the ending letters *m* and *n* are due to dialectal differences which more especially appear in proper names like *Gide'ōn* and *Gide'ōm*, *Ethān* and *Ethām*, etc.

35. On another occasion we shall deal more fully with this tendency of Moses to restrict the rights and privileges of the priests as much as possible, and show how shaky all the combinations are, which Biblical critics heaped around the so-called "development" of priesthood in Israel.

36. See *The Expulsion of the Hyksos* in Journal Eg. Arch., Vol. V (1918) and Gardiner's latest article, *Tanis and Pi-Ramesse*, l.c. Vol. XIX (1933), pp. 127-8, where he confirms again his belief "that the expulsion of the Hyksos [was] the great historical event which gave rise to the story of the oppression and flight."

37. Even in the most recent publications on the early history of Israel the scepticism about the historicity of the Exodus is still maintained (see e.g., the recent last

edition of R. Kittles' *Geschichte des Volkes Israel* in the chapter dealing with Israel in Egypt). The arguments based on an extraordinary amount of research and learning sufficiently justify our statement.

38. For the Israel stela see: J. Breasted, *Records of Ancient Egypt*, III, §§ 602 seq.; for the stela of *Besan:* The Museum Journal, Philadelphia, 1923, p. 245, and *Journal Eg. Arch.*, XIV (1928), p. 280 seq. The identification of *Apiri* with Hebrews has long ago been suggested and substantiated by many quotations from Egyptian texts by Heyes, in his book *Bibel und Aegypten*. The only difficulty lies in the fact that *Apiri* is mentioned in Egyptian texts much earlier than the appearance of the Hebrews; but, as it will be shown on another occasion, this does not render the above identification impossible.

39. The difference in the vocalisation of *Rameses* in Gen. 47[11] and Ex. 12[37], as the name of the district of Goshen, and *Raamses*, as the name of the store city Ex. 1[11], has long ago been noticed. Whether this difference has any foundation or is merely accidental, cannot be decided, as we do not exactly know how the name of the city or of the king was pronounced by the Egyptians. It may be mentioned that the name of the King is reproduced in cuneiform script as *Rameshiya*. As to the site of *Raamses* or *Per-Rameses*, the location is not quite certain. It was believed first by Brugsch that it was in Tanis, the Biblical *Ẕō'an;* this was challenged by A. H. Gardiner, who identified it with Pelusium, by which he upset the whole itinerary of the Exodus, *Journal Eg. Arch.*, V and X. Now in his *Retractation*, in the same *Journal*, XIX (1933), p. 122 sq., he accepts again Brugsch's opinion, which is supported by recent excavations at Tanis, and rehabilitates the Hebrew writer of the Exodus story as being right in having

located Raamses in Tanis. But, as we pointed out, this question is not decisive for the account of the Exodus itself.

40. In some typical cases, such as the tree of life, the serpent and the woman, the ark of Noah, Assyro-Babylonian pictures were added to the Egyptian illustrations in order to show how obvious the presence of Egyptian elements is, and how far away from the real issue the Assyriologists have gone to enforce on Biblical accounts Assyro-Babylonian influence.

41. See note 33. We refer more especially to the manner in which the Egyptian mythology represents the creation of the first divine couple *Shū* and *Tefēnet* and of the body of God the creator, or the creation of the Expansion with the stars out of the bodies of *Nūt* and *Geb*. This and the ways of cunning and ferocious fighting of the gods against each other, beginning with the murder of *Osiris* by his brother *Seth*, give a fair idea of the moral qualities attributed to the great gods and fully justify the contempt and aversion with which the Pentateuch so often refers to the "Egyptian abominations."

42. The *Ka*, the so-called double, was according to Egyptian belief the hidden companion of the living and the dead. His real function consisted in intermediating between the soul (*ba*) and the earthly body, if preserved in the tomb, so that it "comes again to life" as often as the soul descends on it (see illustration p. 156).

43. See Prof. M. Murray's review on *The Lang. of the Pent.* in the *Journal of the Royal Asiatic Society*, 1933, in which she refers to a similar phenomenon in the Granta and Cam rivers in England.

44. It is very important to mention here that the

description (Gen. 2¹²) of the gold as being "good" is not to be taken as a general characterisation of the gold, but as a literal reproduction of a technical term, very common in Egyptian, *nūb nefer*, "good gold," for the finest quality of gold, as distinguished from other kinds of gold such as river gold, white gold, mountain gold, etc. Such precision in the description of the gold can only be explained by the author's familiarity with the products of that region and its river.

45. There is also another Egyptian divinity represented as a serpent called *renenet* bearing also the name "mistress of food" or "mistress of the barn."

46. The customary interpretation of *tehōm* as the Assyro-Babylonian dragon *tihāmat* is especially from a linguistic point of view erroneous and utterly misleading with regard to the whole conception of creation, as shown in *The Lang. of the Pent.*, pp. 127-31. It simply means *ocean*, referring to the chaotic waters in creation and to the world ocean in the flood.

47. On the Asiatic borders of Egypt along the desert on the Suez Canal, there were several such fortresses in Ancient Egypt with towers which were actually named by the Semitic word *migdal* (reproduced in Egyptian script as *miqtar*).

48. From among the considerable number of books and commentaries characteristic for this kind of *mythologising* Biblical accounts are most typical all the works of H. Winckler, H. Gunkel, *Schoepfung und Chaos*, and more especially, A. Jeremias, *Das Alte Testament im Lichte des Alten Orients* (translated also into English). In this book he surpasses all other Pan-Babylonists with his gifts of inexhaustible imagination which carry him to the heights of the Milky Way and to the depths of the Babylonian hell.

226

CPSIA information can be obtained
at www.ICGtesting.com
Printed in the USA
LVHW010110181222
735289LV00005B/482

9 780353 468986